SUMMER HOME REVIEW

A Community of Words
A Circle of Poets

An Anthology of Selected
Poems and Stories

Edited by

Jacqueline M. Loring

ISBN: 1-40331-103-X (Electronic)
ISBN: 1-40331-104-8 (Paperback)

Library of Congress Control Number: 2002103582

This book is printed on acid free paper.

Printed in the United States of America
Bloomington, IN

1stBooks - rev. 06/17/02

Dedication

Without the dreams and the work of many people, the Summer Home Review would still be a sitting in a chair by the ocean, waiting.

Thank you to my husband, Gary, who allowed me to quit my full time day job so I could write and to my mother, children and grandchildren for being there. Thank you to Gary Rafferty who listened longest and whose shove was persistent but soft, to Pauline Hebert, my inspiration, for her heart of gold, to Preston Hood whose words kept me working and for being here when I needed him, to Catherine Sasanov whose knowledge and logic kept me going in a straight line, to David Connolly for always being a "brat", to Dorinda Foley Wegener for the beautiful way she expresses her words and 'our' ideas and for bringing us Scott and baby Emma, to Berred, Dominique, Adrienne, Carrie and Jessica for joining our hands, to Steffanie Schwam for her faith, and to all the poets and writers whose work is included, thank you for believing.

Thank you to Dana Nelson and Joyce Keay for their skills, to my poetry guru, Sheila Whitehouse, to Ginger Robinson for the years of friendship and unwavering approval, Norma McAuliffe for giving me back my days and to Clare Chandler, my sister, for always finding time to listen to a poem, or edit a page and the courage to smile through the last couple of months. And to my friend, Dianne Ouellette, thank you for waiting just long enough, without you this Review would still be a summer thought.

Prologue

Summer Home Review Anthology is a literary labyrinth, an honoring of the written word, and a dream come true.

The circle of poets and writers herein are nurses, researchers, firemen, high school and college teachers, healers, artists, soldiers, lawyers, singers, doctors, union members, playwrights, and entrepreneurs. They have in common their participation at the same writers' workshop. Some of the poets are strangers; some know each other's names and some are friends. One poet has passed. While it is true that some of the poets are Vietnam veterans, this editor does not want the reader to assume that this book is either "war" poetry or writing that is of "workshop" quality. All the poems in Summer Home Review have an edge. Over the past thirteen years, I have attended writing conferences, workshops, classes, and courses and participated in many writing groups. The William Joiner Center for the Study of War and Social Consequence, UMass Boston, Boston, Massachusetts is just one of those experiences but it is the one Summer Home Review celebrates.

My path to this anthology evolved like a labyrinth, bending back upon itself, growing, including an ever-widening circle of friends and always winding toward this book. My journey began in the unlikeliest of places with the war in Vietnam.

In the fall of 1988, my oldest daughter entered her senior year in high school. Though she had an early acceptance to the college of her choice, she still had two projects she needed to complete. Her English paper was due in April of 1989 and her 4-H Visual Presentation was scheduled for February.

As the oldest daughter of a Vietnam veteran, it might be expected that her choice for the topic "War in Vietnam" of her senior paper and that for her 4-H project she would choose "Vietnam, the County" which it was. But in our house, in 1989, Vietnam was never mentioned.

Our family was comprised of biological, adopted and foster children who knew the "fact" that their father served in Vietnam. One night at dinner a child asked him if he had ever killed anyone. My husband replied that during his "good tour" he worked in a hospital, had not "seen combat", had not "carried a gun" and no, he had never "killed anyone". Even children understand the silence that followed.

For her senior paper research, my daughter talked with experts on the war. The University of Massachusetts in Boston had a center for the Study of War and Social Consequence called the William Joiner Center. Jaime Rodriguez and David Hunt gave her interviews and supplied her with statistics and reading material. It was later that year that I heard the name of the Joiner Center again.

According to a flyer at the Vietnam Veteran's Out-reach Center in Hyannis, the Joiner Center was sponsoring their 2nd Annual Writers' Conference. I arrived at UMass for orientation hot and stressed but determined to juggle my work and family life. Lost in the maze of the under campus parking garage I spotted a car with a bumper sticker from a restaurant on Martha's Vineyard and one from the Hyannis Outreach Center. I followed the lanky, blond man through the parking lot, into an elevator to a room in the Wheatly building with a registration desk and 35 people. During orientation, T. Michael Sullivan and Kevin Bowen discussed the format of the two-week conference and introduced the faculty. Among the names I didn't know were O'Brien, Rottmann, Heinemann, Steptoe, Ehrhart, and Karlin. The faculty explained the individual workshops and read their class list. A tall, handsome man with a dimple in his chin said he was Bruce Weigl. The last name read was mine. He paused and said, "All the poets come with me." For a moment I couldn't move. "Me, a poet?" I joined Chris Gompert, the man from Martha's Vineyard and for the next two weeks I studied with Bruce who continues to be an inspiration for me in ways he cannot imagine.

The conference unfolded in a blur of confusion, raw edged emotion and a sense of heightened energy. Almost all of the 1980s and early 1990s Joiner Center faculty and attendees had a connection to the war in Vietnam. On the second day of class, I read a poem that identified me as the wife of a vet. From that point on the veterans in the class, Chris Gompert, Patrick Harrington, Roger Martin and Preston Hood, took me under their wings. They waited for me after class, invited me sit with them at lunch, and made arrangements for me to join them at evening poetry readings. That first year, when my poems were a series of desperate thoughts about the stress of living in the aftermath of war, they supported and nourished me in the way children care for a lost puppy.

I grew up in the protection of a loving family in the closely-knit neighborhood in an Irish Catholic parish in Dorchester, Massachusetts. As I entered high school, we moved to the suburbs where I was thrown into a class of over 500. I remember the cocoon of my childhood. In my adult life I never recovered that sense of belonging until I sat with those men at the 1989 faculty poetry reading at the Phillip Brooks House at Harvard University. That night we crushed into the leather couches of the mahogany room to hear Lamont Steptoe, Tim O'Brien, Larry Rottmann, Larry Heinemann, Bill Ehrhart, Wayne Karlin and Bruce Weigl. During the readings, I cried as I shared their pain and loss. I watched them read and care for each other. I saw the tenderness in Wayne Carlin's hands as he held and soothed the very tired baby boy of one of the readers. That night, for the first time, I heard Bruce Weigl read *Song of Napalm*. A line from that poem changed me forever. "…and not your good love" began a path to discovery that has positively affected my life to this day.

Over the last thirteen years I have attended workshops at the Joiner Center with a who's who of contemporary literature including Yusef Komunyakaa, Fred Marchant, and Bruce Weigl. I have studied poetry with W.D. Ehrhart, fiction with Larry Heinemann, and word discipline with Tim O'Brien (and yes, T. Michael, I survived that two weeks!). I learned courage from Carolyn Forche, play writing from Ed Bullins, worked on translations with Martha

Collins and was challenged to write about peace from Lady Borton and Lee Swenson. Christian Langworthy taught me hear the voice of our children. I have been inspired by Daisy Zamora, charmed by Grace Paley, and grateful for the opportunity to learn from Vietnamese poets and writers and to hear them read their work. I was blessed to spend a day on Martha's Vineyard with Claribel Alegria. As the years have passed since the early 1990s, the faculty at the Joiner Center has evolved to include writers from all over the world like John Deane and Eva Bourke. I look forward to the opportunity in the future to work with faculty like Doug Anderson, Marilyn Nelson, Demetria Martinez, George Evans, Keith Wilson, Martin Espada, Michael Casey and others.

In June of 1990, among my responsibilities as co-chair with Bill Silver-Ryder of the Cape and Island Nam Vet's *"Moving Wall"* Committee, was the opening and closing ceremonies. With the support of many including W.D. Ehrhart and Larry Lee Rottmann, the Center sponsored a community wide poetry contest. The winners read at the closing ceremonies along with the invited readers Preston Hood, Patrick Harrington, Roger Martin and Chris Gompert and featured reader, Lamont B. Steptoe.

Poetry courses, workshops and/or classes are different from writing groups where there is a facilitator or "guru" who is not the group teacher. Participants pass out poems for the group to read and critique and then workshopped poems are returned. Writer's workshops share many similarities but at a conference course, class or workshop there is an instructor and the participants expect to learn. My first workshop in 1989 is the template I use for workshop success. The structure is simple. The teacher teaches. Poets bring poems to be workshopped. With the support and expertise of the instructor, a poem is discussed while the poet listens. For the workshop novice the experience can be a sublime examination of one's talent or it can be difficult or even excruciatingly painful. For the seasoned workshop goer it can be an ego killer or an affirmation. Either way, if the instructor has made the class environment safe, great poems are born and friendships begin. Over the years, I have penciled my comments on poems and dutifully returned them. I confess, though, there have been times when I loved or hated a poem so intensely that I slipped it under the pile on my desk to hide its abduction from the writer and the instructor. I love work I can remember, words or lines I can't wait to repeat. Unfortunately, I remember lines better than I remember who wrote them. Giving credit is difficult years after hearing a great line or stanza. In my 1990 Gloria Emerson class a student read a hysterically funny, short story about living in his van. I wish I had kept my copy, or could remember David's last name. I do remember my 1991 Yusef Komunyakaa workshop included Gary Rafferty, Maureen Ryberg and Kevin Bowen. A young woman read a poem I still think about. During a mid-morning break, she told classmates how the poem came to be written. She said she was sitting in a toilet stall at Filenes's when suddenly, instinctively, she knew the woman in the next stall was her biological mother who she had never met. Unlike Sue Robert's poem, "To the Children I Will Never Have", I gave my copy back.

It is not uncommon for students to gather, bind and distribute the collected works of their class. In August of 2001, Steffanie Schwam printed a booklet from Fred Marchant's course at the Cape Cod Writers' Conference. I prize my spiral bound anthology from Eva Bourke's 1998 Joiner Center class (thanks Bob!), the beautiful, class written poem from my 1996 Daisy Zamora class, and my collection of abducted poems.

Within the past 2 or 3 years, I've noticed that conferences themselves have joined the growing list of readers who recognize the publishable quality of the writing done at their workshops. The Sun Coast Writer's Conference at the University of Florida and the Maui Screen Writer's workshop in Hawaii offer works by their participants for sale.

Still, many conference poems are abandoned. As writers know the business of getting work published is a job separate from the inspiration and as difficult as putting words on a page. Many poets will never walk the path to publication and some great poems never leave a workshop notebook. Researching literary journals and magazines is a time consuming, learning experience as is finding small publishing houses or university presses that will read manuscripts from unpublished poets. Getting a poem into an anthology can be an impossible task. You have to be published to be published! For some unknown poets inclusion in a major anthology comes only from the generosity of known ones. In 1998, Gary Rafferty, David Connolly, Pauline Hebert and I were included in the Scribner

Anthology, *From Both Sides Now The Poetry of the Vietnam War and its Aftermath*, edited by Phillip Mahony, through the generosity and willingness to share publishing opportunities of Lamont Steptoe and W.D. Ehrhart.

How many fine poems never see the light of poetic day because their owners write to write but not to publish? I know poets who are so shy about their creative worth or about the event that led to the poem's inspiration that they refuse to send their 'babies' into the forest. It is a sad fact that hidden in the midst of those crumpled up, thrown away copies, or the plastic covered, student generated conference booklets, there may well be a great poem, the next Pulitzer Prize winning poet, or Poet Laureate, or the writer of the next best seller. Read the work of Dorinda Foley Wegener and Carmi Soifer in Summer Home Review. But writer's conferences have drawbacks. Writers high on the creative energy generated by working with a brilliant teacher in a talented, group of poets, leave workshops to return on Monday to their unpoetic lives. What happens to the pieces of poems that remain?

In the summer of 1996, after an especially draining two weeks working with Tim O'Brien, I invited several poets to the Cape for a weekend. Personally, I needed to corral the poems refusing to settle quietly into the summer home of my mind. I knew other poets were suffering the effects of the intensity of the Joiner Center, too. That July, we struggled all weekend with unfinished poems, leaving lines in notebooks to be crafted into poems over the winter. From the summer of 1996 to this last one, our group has grown, our poetry has matured, but our weekend ritual remains. Poets arrive from Friday morning to Sunday night. We read, critique, rewrite, discuss, and rewrite poems. We circle our chairs and move them as the sun rises over the hedge in the side yard. We work till the sun at our backs sets into the ocean. Dinner is always at sunset on the porch of a local restaurant or at a picnic table on Back River. Friday flows into Sunday. New poems rest till the Joiner Center in June.

In 1998 and 1999, Dorinda Foley Wegener, Pauline Hebert, Preston Hood, Gary Rafferty and I first discussed an anthology of Joiner Center participants. In 2000, the first organized attempt at a bound anthology of our poems resulted in a booklet used at readings at the Sanford Vet's Center, Sanford, Maine and at the Bourne Library, Bourne Massachusetts and included poems by David Connolly. In 2001, at Gary Rafferty's kitchen table, in Catherine Sasanov's living room and in Dianne Ouellette's dining room plans for professionally published anthology were considered and Summer Home Review and Summer Home Press were born. Flyers announcing the anthology were available at the 2001 Joiner Center Workshop. The response was immediate. This book is the result.

For the poets and writers in this book, I would like to express my gratitude to T. Michael Sullivan and to Kevin Bowen for their work to sustain the Joiner Center Writer's Conference, occasionally against great odds. Our poems thank you.

For the reader, it is my hope that as you turn the pages of this book, you will delight in a poem that might have remained in notebook or that you will hate a poem enough to recite it or give it to a friend. I hope you will be able to trace our common literary bonds and friendships through our work. My photos will help. You may be able to follow the trail of Bruce Weigl's influence or that of Fred Marchant, Yusef Komunyakaa, Lady Borton, Eva Bourke, or Martha Collins. I think you'll discover the respect and awe we have for each other and for our teachers.

Each path we took as poets and writers to the poems and stories included in this anthology is similar to the experience of walking the sacred path of the labyrinth. Like pilgrims in a labyrinth, the poets and writers included in this book have reached the center and, with publication of this book, are making their way back to the beginning. This book begins for you at the center. Walk with us. In between the lines we have left for you sacred pieces of ourselves. Enjoy your journey.

Jacqueline Murray Loring

Table of Contents

xvi

List of Photos

Introduction

Summer Home Review is the dream of Dianne Collins Ouellette and Jacqueline Loring. Having attended many conferences, workshops, and poetry readings, they suddenly found themselves writing poetry. In the art of writing, particularly poetry, there is a satisfaction of expression in words, with few rules, that reveal the truth. That is, the writer believes strongly in the ability to use words to; persuade the reader, to evoke emotions, to extract humor, and to entertain. Summer Home Review brings this revelation to anyone who will read and listen. Yes, listen! Read some of these poems aloud. Listen to the sound of the words, the inflection of the voice. The human voice is the most personal of musical instruments. Musicians speak of the search for expression. In jazz, for instance, the melody, be it notes on a piano or lyrics from a singer, is meant to sound conversational, personal. While Dianne was working on her studies at the University of Massachusetts, Amherst, she was inspired by the poetry she had read, which turned into a desire to write poetry. As Preston Hood says—" Soon she found the place that all poets strive to reach, where poems just are, without explanation." And so it is with the writers in this book. Thanks to the help of poetry groups, workshops, and teachers, this book has become a reality. Dianne and Jackie are inspired by a new awareness of poetry and the response it brings from the readers. In this response, they have succeeded in fulfilling their dream.

Richard Berred Ouellette

Summer Home – Cape Cod, Massachusetts, 2001

Section 1.

…alone before words
Carmi Soifer, *Template*

Gary Rafferty, Boston, Massachusetts, University of Massachusetts, 2000, Reading from Anthologies, *From Both Sides Now* and *Between the Lines*, at Joiner Center

Empty House
Gary Rafferty

The pink kitchen cabinets stand
with their mouths open.

Bedrooms, once full of children,
inhabited by ghosts of furniture
outlined on the wallpaper.

Hallways, the temporary province of spiders.

In the living room
the sun probes hollow
through filmy windowpanes.

Chairmarks on the wide pine floorboards
like the dimples of a hammer
from a careless carpenter,

On the piano,
pushed up against the wall
a metronome pleads
for the touch of a finger

**Sue Roberts and Grace Paley, Boston, Massachusetts,
University of Massachusetts, 2001, Joiner Center**

Poem for the Children I Will Never Give Birth To
Sue Roberts

I will never know you, feel your pull and tug,
the soft mantle of your heads against me.

You will never drop eggs, whose puzzles you ask me
to explain; there will be no messes to sponge from the
floor.

I will not hear you shift at night, turning beneath sheets
you picked
out, the ones I wouldn't have chosen but you claimed
you had to have.

I will not fold your clothes or arrange the books you've
spilled
on the carpet, or move your bicycles from behind the
car in the drive.

I will never sit in the second row of your grammar
school auditorium
waiting to register your three-line speech with a flash.

Does this yearning, this inner gulf, want a child to fill
it?
Would my dangerous darknesses recede if I put a child
at the center?

I will have to understand the choices I've made,
which did not include you, although I've dreamed of
you often.

I hope you will forgive my solitary life, the one I
morticed
from pain and grief, the one I struggled to build and
have grown to love.

It is not that I was unwilling to know you; it was
simply easier,
in a world of so many hungry mouths, to feed only my
own,

holding my heart like a small bird against the storm.
It was all I could do, and it is enough.

Sinner in the Hands
Dianne Ouellette

I performed an act of contrition every day.
Bored with God stories, I thought of them as
    Nancy Drew mysteries:
The Secret of the Lost Temple,
The Mysterious Burning Bush.
Sister Mary Francis sent me to Mother Superior;
ah, another student to mete out acts of Hail Marys.
Kneel here, she said;
I touched the green velvet hand rest.
I was not alone in that place;
He looked down from every corner,
I spoke to him,
gave him a litany of my joy.
At Easter, crawling with the other 7-year-old sinners,
I believed I was the queen
captured by the devil himself—
by my muteness I would save my people.
God was in me then;
I've never been holier.
I was compelled to believe,
yet silenced by disbelief.
Every time I spoke,
the good nun said to stand in the corner,
arms above my head.
My arms became strong.
I learned to tell stories.
The plots were thin at first,
but I learned the craft,
the art,
thanks be to God.

The Test
Jacqueline M. Loring

The wood door slams,
sharp as the ruler's sting,
silences all.

My younger sister's braids
tumble off her woolen shoulders,
escape the nun's prod.

As she recites my four times table
from under straight cut bangs,
my sister's tears warm my classroom,

find the last row seat
where I concentrate
on my rosary

beads, entwined
among burning finger tips
and thumbs that touch

to form an A
above
my fifth grade failure.

**Carmi Soifer and John Deane, Boston, Massachusetts,
University of Massachusetts, 2000, Joiner Center**

Template
Carmi Soifer

Once I saw my grandfather
show affection: *Gooseberries,*
he said, *I like these.*

Now winter disguises the tall white stone,
marks where a path might be, a way
my parents hiked before marriage.

It's dusk, I am lying in the place before sleep,
listening to bugs and the sounds of children
somewhere, *katy did, katy didn't.*

I alone am alone, before language.
Fog floods my stomach;
promises a habit of fog.

Air black with stars, roofs of trees
shifting weight in the wind.
All I know of prayer, permission

is folded in the brown
morning smell of oatmeal, served warm
in round bowls made of earth.

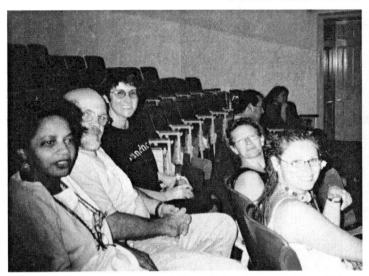

Group of students: seated, left to right, top row: MaryEdna Salvi, Preston Hood, Catherine Sasanov, seated, left to right, first row: Dorinda Foley Wegener, Dianne, Ouellette, Cambridge, Massachusetts, 2001 Joiner Center faculty reading at Harvard University

Tryptich: Blue
MaryEdna Salvi

1.

Three colors painted in wide bands
across the canvas.
Pastels? Maybe.
The tones are hushed.
Still, they glisten behind
the little girl in the white dress
with black hair and blue skin.

She carries a basket on her arm.
A hand is raised to her mouth
and the head is bent just a bit.
One more step to take
and she will walk out of the picture.

2.

Daddy's here visiting.
I'm home, 'cause I'm
not feeling well.

Crayons and coloring book
are on the kitchen table.
We never sit like this. Just daddy
and me? We don't talk. Just color.

I look over to see his picture.
It's so beautiful.
Daddy has colored the cow on his page blue.

I ask him why.
"When you color, you
can do anything you want." He leaves.

My cousin Kathy has come over.
I show the picture. She laughs at it.

3.

The little girl in the white dress
with black hair and blue skin
alone and carefree,
walks barefoot
the basket swings on her arm
she fills it with her own
thoughts and dreams.

Lisa Fay, Dianne Ouelette and Fred Marchant (standing), Boston, Massachusetts, University of Massachusetts, 2000

Nursing Home Necklace
Lisa Fay

I wear my name necklace
my niece made for me
and my friend all of 80
with no hair and teeth
uses her farm hands
to pull off my necklace,
hard as a fisherman reeling in the net.

Now you leave me breathless,
robbed of a heirloom,
not wanting to be
the daughter you wished for.

News
Maureen Ryberg
(Ni Chonaill)

Rain drizzles out the lines of the horizon,
paints a gray expanse of emptiness
winding sheet white. Little bits of shale

shudder their way back to shore.
A lone seagull floats in its element,
one yellow eye scanning the beach

for carcasses. All that is left
of the fishermen's cottages
are foundation stones, sinking

deep in the long grass. Inside
the twelve-foot square that limned their lives,
by the hearth where her grandmother

boiled kettle after kettle of water
and waited for news,
I made Mother stand for a photo.

Wind buffeted her frail, resisting form,
sucked the ends of her woolen scarf
skywards. The ocean breathes

with its mouth open; it inhales, exhales
souls. I see the *curragh* drifting back
without the men, without

her beloved Eugene; fish scales gleam
on its greening boards; the gunwale is smashed.
When they took the boat apart they found

the nailmarks of the missing men
under the wooden seat. What was I hoping
to recreate? Mother knew their ghosts

had abandoned this strip of land.
The dead have the right to remain
silent as the rain that's falling out to sea,

deaf, as God is, to the cries of the suffering,
blind to the inch-by-inch erosion of the waves.
I scoop up a briny mouthful, spit it out.

At my feet, a perfect seashell, alabaster pink,
the color painted on with wind and spume
to make me sigh for news from other worlds.

In my ear, fossil-music, like a hymn
to what is gone, what is to come—
God does nothing. He makes the nothing sing.

Food for Thought, 3:00 AM
David Connolly

They move in unison
like dancers in a ballet,
the spider, twenty inches from my rifle,
the VC, twenty feet further out, in line,
each slowly sliding a leg forward.
I let the man take one more step
so as not to kill the bug.

Sarah Furo, Boston, Massachusetts, University of Massachusetts, Boston, 1999

The Mysteries
Sarah Furo

I.
Kore

Here is the story told many times,
the tale of the girl, Persephone,
her mother, and the sudden
disappearance of that sweet child
into the deep embrace of Hades.

Demeter, Mother of all,
wise and fruitful
grew distraught
with the disappearance of her daughter.
She tore her robes—
young apple trees in blossom on the hill,
yanked out her long and shining hair—
wheat blowing in the fields.
She screamed, and fainted and despaired.

Demeter alone among the Great Ones,
did not know Persephone
held sway in a kingdom of her own.

She wandered, ashen, crazed,
and took a turn at caring
for another woman's child
until that mother observed
her nursemaid dipping the babe
into the fires of immortality.

Screaming, the mortal queen
drove out our Great Mother
from her hearth,
only to be crushed
by the sight of the Goddess,
taller than any oak tree
rising up from the rags
       of her disguise.

Demeter's distress
beat upon the earth.
She who made all in joy,
in sorrow, left all to die.

Meanwhile, beneath
the brown breast
of the Mother
who wept for her,
Persephone fell in step
to the ways of the dark kingdom.

Hades, ruler of the underworld,
she knew as husband and lord.

Was Persephone Maiden or Queen?
One ruby seed from her mother's
fruit, as it passed between her lips,
Lips swollen with kisses,
condemned her to
return to Pluto's palace.
Was it promise or sentence
to her husband's realm?

At last the cruel hoax was halted.
Persephone was wrapped
in the loving arms of her mother.
All was set right
and our earth rejoiced
in the maiden's return.

Exiled from her dark realm
each springtime,
Persephone wanders
through the fruitful earth
apple blossoms in her hair
pomegranate in her mouth.

II.
Hades

Upon her sudden entrance
to the Kingdom of the Dead,
the childlike Persephone
was transformed,
her light stripped away.

For no maiden
may walk the halls of Hades.
Yet the story does not end here,
in shame and loss.

While the gateway was harsh,
the castle was full of pleasures,
and Persephone came to cherish
the shadowless towers,

the rolling dark meadows,
and strange fruit and flowers.

Those who have not traveled these lands
should not speak of their imagined gloom.

She who had once run carefree,
a flower by her mother's side,
now walked with purpose,
her household in awe
of her quiet gaze.

Never forget it was she,
the maiden, now queen,
who allowed Orpheus,
musician to the gods,
to seek out his beloved
in the deep valleys
of the shadowy dead.
The tender heart of Persephone
prevailed upon her lord
to release the bride
to the bridegroom,
a reminder that what
cannot be mended
in this world,
may come together
in the next.

III.
Aphrodite

In the core of our apple,

we call the planet earth,
dwells the great polestar
of the underworld-
Lord of Change,
Transformer eternal,
Hades himself.

With each breath
he draws into his lungs
the Universe is born anew.
His trumpet voice penetrates
where justice has been forgotten.
Hades alone has the key
to every rusted lock.

Why then,
is it scowling Hades
Lady Aphrodite,
bright and beautiful,
so lightly appointed
for the maiden,
Persephone—to be her
chosen spouse?

Whoever has walked
across a freshly plowed
field at twilight
and raised loving eyes
to see the crescent
moon adorned
by the evening star,
you are entering
the drama which

has no beginning
and knows no end.

Once more the Maiden
returns pure and slender
to be gathered like wheat
in the brown arms
of her grieving mother.

Once more we are freed
from the dark shelter
of womb and grave.

**Connie Veenendall & Maureen Ryberg, Boston
Massachusetts, University of Massachusetts, Boston, 2001**

Tree Swallows
Cornelia Veenendaal

Against the cold sky,
indigo head, white breast, slate
along the wings, not a feather stirs,
near the crooked, weather-beaten
birdhouse, the dry stalks.

Suddenly the bird is in the sky,
a widening compass,
zigzagging into the far trees,
his sharp signal comes back
across the meadow.

Out of the birdhouse
the brown mate arrows,
I hear the clip clip of her wings;
I leave the rampant garden
and walk back to the house,

to its friends and presences.
There is fire in the hearth.
The birdguide names them:
Tree Swallows.
I have forgotten my bitterness.

Three daughters arrive;
they begin planting, and I help them,
with wheelbarrow and water jugs.
All day they work, like their Frisian
forebears. They get covered in mud

and say unexpected, flying things.
At the table at night, one says,
"I've known you for a hundred years,
but never really known you
until today."

Tender Morsels
Jacqueline M. Loring

Inside his mind,
my father searches
his life's
menu. With words
that trickle
like syrup
over the top
of thoughts
he struggles
to stack
sentences
to nourish me
before his banquet
passes.

My Hands, a Mix
E. B. Moore

Patriarchal palm hammered square. Fingers
nearly mannish saved by narrowed bone,
mothered moons, crescent filings.

Hatch-marks, might be mine, cross lines:
paternal life calloused short; maternal heart
and head splice to a well-rope let down,
the touch-filled bucket drawn—

grandmother, mother, to me,
handed down. Hands I pass on.
Pulse at the wrists mine. Mine
for now.

Returning
Steffanie Schwam

Your beauty incises my chest,
into deep canyons of heart wood.

Who knew your scalpel would be
a pink lady's slipper, nodding in the May breeze?

What am I to do with this terrible gift?
I crumble at the lady's feet.

I have turned too often to give others ease;
unable to free my own deepest woe.

A hush washes through me and into those who suffer;
it streams along my breath, intention, touch, word.

There must be more than suffering to bring me close,
to bring me fully into love again.

I stopped loving when you died, mother.
My heart fled with your last breath.

I massaged your dreadfully decaying back,
fed you Haagen-Dazs coffee ice cream.

With each touch, each wooden spoonful,
your bliss spilled out, filling the room.

Now, I can touch your green body in the brook,
hear you whisper that I helped your crossing.

I carry your legacy within,
a thimble of your nectar.

Preserves
Peg Mahoney

I.

In late summer of 1947, before I return to school,
my grandmother and I pick grapes
from a tangle of vines and nettles behind our house,
examine each orb for bruises or beak marks.
In the yellow kitchen, we wash and squeeze
ripe fruit through our fingers
toss by handfuls into the scoured jelly kettle.
Grandma scoops in sugar, fresh spices, powdered
    pectin.
The mixture bubbles as we take turns stirring.
She skims off
the amethyst frost
sieves molten liquid
into a cluster of sterile jars waiting for their fill.

I pour hot paraffin onto each portion
then pack the year's yield into cartons
to be padlocked in the cellar's storage room
until each jar is ceremoniously awarded
to aunts and neighbors and special friends.
In the spattered kitchen
we celebrate our annual ritual
with a pot of Bewleys's tea
and scones slathered with hot jam.

II.

In late summer of 1950,
grackles invade our back yard
bursting open the last bountiful harvest.
Shriveled skins linger among the nettles,
haunting reminders of once-luscious fullness.

III.

In late summer of 1995,
my grandchild visits before she returns to school.
We splatter lined white paper with purple markers
as we write poems and stories,
sip chamomile tea
nibble scones slathered with store bought jam.
I tell her about my grandmother's spirit,
measureless,
and how she preserved my childhood.

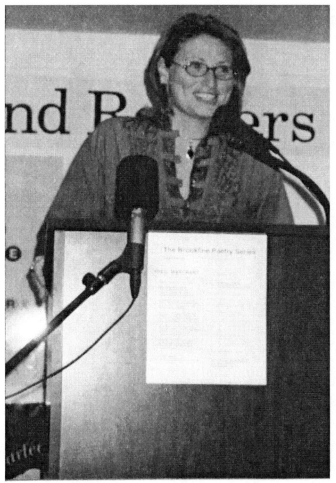

Dorinda Foley Wegener, Brookline, Massachusetts, Brookline Booksmith, 2001, Reading at Night of Women Readers

Nana's Arms
Dorinda Foley Wegener

On Harrison Street resides an apartment, old
as Saint Patrick's Cathedral.
The dark mahogany stairs, each a church pew,
lead me to an eight year old heaven.
I rush down the hall, anticipate
a *wonderful, wonderful* evening of Lawrence Welk.

The gates swing open.
She stands in the frame.
The God rays burst through the window,
silhouette her form in heavenly grace.

I yell *Pro-pell-ahhh!*
She raises her arms out, stretches
them wide. The skin and muscles on her upper arms
    hangs
low like inverted angel wings.
She begins to shake those heavy arms, makes airplane
    noises.
I squeal as I watch her under arms jiggle and swing
like Tommy Dorsey, Nat King Cole, or a gospel
choir singing praises to the Lord.
Those winged arms would swoop down, pick me up.
Hug me tight in an angelic embrace.
Nana's arms, those Rubens limbs
lift me up to the Lord.

Deliver me to all the graces
of heaven, PB&J's, Donny and Marie paper dolls,
and the my-size pillow with red rose buds, the tag
'With love from Nana'.

A Peony the Moon Leans Toward
Preston Hood
(for Jake)

It was in your words, your tone
the kindness to ask us to read
at Cambridge College, share
our souls together, mixing like
blood brother/sister paint. You said,
"I want us to wring out the wet
conditioning of fears spilled from the years,
people need to know things worth feeling.
They need to know the reliving, the churning,
the rubble of our fragile selves, the deep
silence in the blackest Nam war."

Wife vet, sister, mother
hanging in there with us all,
pulling us out of loneliness into love.

You read first, after your introduction,
Song of Napalm, a poem by Bruce Weigl.
The stage was set for our catharsis
what we once lost: each reading
each sigh, every sliver of tear held
each into a different kind of light
so the audience upon feeling sad
hears the waves inside the soul's wounds.

Listening, we hear from your voice
the poems natural flow, the inner
character of what you wanted to say, you said.
It wasn't a lie, it didn't swing back.

From your nod and deepest voice
you carried all Nam's secrets
& sufferings away from us
like a heron in deep wood
shuttling her young to safety.

For one brief moment, your insistence
gave us spirit & we felt
these first days of March
the blur of distance closing
the fire is out, the stars.

We circle in words in hands:
Jake. Lamont. Gary.
Preston. Dorinda. Pauline.
We cast our shadows as poems

our wounds, woes, our words
are skipping stones on flat seas.

Be a reader, a child story teller
sound your soul, be
a bearer of gifts, Jake.

Another Woman's Cologne
MaryEdna Salvi

She puts her hands into the hot water
scrubs the tiles, scrubs the porcelain,
her face reflects back to her
just like on TV.
Only she's not smiling and she's not wearing
pearl earrings and high heels.

She dusts the tops, the crevices, the swirls
the legs, and the bottoms
of every piece of furniture.

My mother breathes in
the odor of lemon-scented polish
like other women sniff
their favorite cologne.

Unsure
Pauline Hebert

I don't know the precise moment
when frozen cubes began to tumble
through my ventricles
when soul eclipsed my body

I don't know the precise moment
when brain re-set my internal clock
when reality would forevermore click
out of synchrony

leaving me an emotional pauper

Perhaps
there was one too many rounds
one too many med-evacs flown
one too many casualties

Perhaps
there was no other way
to stay alive.

Year after year I return each today
to the only Vietnam I know
hold my breath
mentally fly med-evacs
knuckles white
on my Toyota's steering wheel.

**Grace Paley and Candace Perry, Boston, Massachusetts,
University of Massachusetts, 2001, after student reading at
Joiner Center**

Your Family
Candace Perry

You have never been a man to make trouble. You did as told to survive the camps, and after. No argument with the Hebrew Immigrant Aid Society, no demand for New York, Statue of Liberty. Instead, New Orleans, Louisiana, the HIAS tells you. Tulane University, jazz, streetcars named "Desire."

The Jews in New Orleans welcome you. They live in white mansions on Saint Charles Avenue, have black servants, run the museums. All they know of sorrow is that they cannot be kings and queens of Mardi Gras.

You are invited to many dinners. The presidents of both reform temples serve shrimp and oysters; no one wears a yarmulke. You could be in Berlin, except for the heat. The wives seat you next to a daughter or niece, students at Sophie Newcomb. The young women mistake you for a professor and blush. You are then twenty-two years old by the calendar, but after four years in Auschwitz...you smile when they complain of the rigors of university life. You progress quickly from student to assistant, a Ph.D. in easy reach.

Her name is Shira, and she looks at you across the crystal goblets without blushing. She is studying pottery, so her fingernails are not painted like the others. When you make love her hold on you is firm, and in those moments you imagine she will remake you into a vessel capable of holding wine, water, hot cocoa.

At your engagement party Shira's father gives a toast, welcomes you to the family. He raises his fluted glass high with one hand and with the other makes a sweeping gesture which requires that he turn his generous body to take in all the people in the room who belong to him. Parents, children, grandchildren, aunts, uncles, nieces, nephews, cousins, servants. You excuse yourself to find the bathroom. Alone, you imitate his gesture and turn – my family, my family, my family – your image in the mirror over the sink all you have left.

You find Shira pulling pots from the kiln the next day. You give her no explanation. She hurls her creations one by one across the studio to smash against the cement block wall. When their warm ashes have settled like bones and nothing remains to break, she concludes it must be another woman and lets you go.

After Shira, you turn down dinner invitations from Jewish community leaders, quit going to meetings of the New Americans Club. You study, listen to jazz, find easy women. Katherine is a secretary in your department. She hears of your broken engagement, invites you to her little apartment for a home cooked meal. She hopes the green beans are okay, back home in Mississippi they always fixed them with ham hocks, but of course she didn't...she never knew any Jews in Mississippi. Her talk is comfortable. She waits until morning to admit you are her first. You confess you would enjoy bacon with your eggs. You know she thinks there is more to it, and you are careful to remain formal and polite at school. When Katherine becomes pregnant, the chairman of your department says you must marry her.

Katherine surprises you with her conversion. None of her family attends your wedding ceremony.

When your daughter is born, Katherine wants to know if there is a family name you would like. Your mother, sisters? Sarah. Rachael. Hannah. How could your mouth speak these names, attach them to daily living, without smoke rising? Brush your teeth, do your homework, I love you. No, you cannot. Katherine chooses Ruth, the convert.

You are offered a teaching position at a small college in Ohio. Katherine tries to contact her family before leaving, but they will have nothing to do with her. On the train, you hold Ruth while Katherine fusses with the baggage and greets the other passengers. You imagine your father's terror. You do not sleep as the topography outside your window changes from wetlands to foothills.

Katherine wants other children. You refuse. You know the math of it. One child can be hidden, smuggled out, kept safe with a neighbor. But this is America, Katherine tries, over and over. Your mother laughed at Germany's little man until it was too late. You think you will not be caught unprepared.

All the years growing up, Ruth wants to know more about the numbers on your forearm, your family, Germany. You teach her to speak perfect German and tell her as little as possible. When Katherine is drinking too much, you and Ruth can have a conversation without interruption. Nazis are allowed to march outside of Chicago. You make sure Ruth always has a full tank of gas and plenty of cash in her pocket. Danke, danke, she laughs, but takes the folded bills you press on her. She is a good daughter. She tries to fix Katherine's problem, she protests wars and other bad behaviors in the world.

Still, you are shocked to silence when Ruth tells you she has fallen in love with a man whose father was in the SS. They are in a group together, children of survivors and children of...now grown, these children think they will remake the world. He is from Berlin. They will have a child. This cannot be your family.

Section II.

…in the long throat of subways
Catherine Sasanov, *Fliers*

Dianne Ouellette, Boston, Massachusetts, University of Massachusetts, 2000, Student reading at Joiner Center

Begin Again Persephone
Dianne Collins Ouellette

I should have known, there were warning signs
but I only knew

orgasms, birth pains, daily life.
I had no language for cancer.

On this train I sleep, read, think,
hope to remember my voice

to come back to life,
hope I've nurtured death long enough.

Fields flash past, wheels grind forward.
This is what I need to know:

each day will lead into another
each day I can feel hunger.

At New London a beautiful woman
boards, sits across from me, falls asleep.

I want to know what her life is like
tell her about mine, but she sleeps,

and the man behind me speaks
to someone far away.

We hurtle past Coop City
Throgs Neck Bridge

past all that laundry, hung out
all those lives, all those years

I've lived without seeing.
Underground now, into the city.

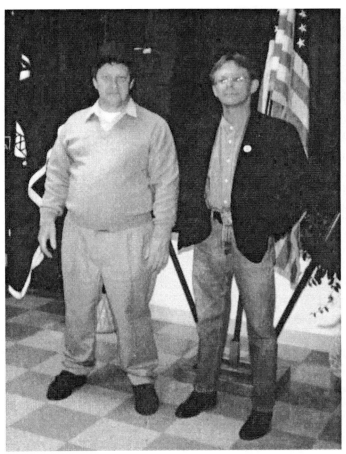

**David Connolly & Gary Rafferty, Hyannis, Mass. Nam Vets
Out-reach Centers, 1995, Reading for Veteran's Day**

For the Medics, the Cops, the Jakes, and America
David Connolly

I've huddled with my brothers,
scared, sweating bullets
in the steam of too many jungle trails,
waiting fretfully for the word
that would send us back into harm's way.

I've moved with those brave men
into some of the dark corners and side rooms of hell,
where shot and shell so suddenly and so utterly
transformed them into broken boys.

And I've heard too many of them
speak the names of wives, of mothers, of god,
as their spirits, given for love of country,
for love of each other, for love of you,
slipped like their blood through our fingers.

So, forgive me for saying so,
but my ears may pick up echoes of some of the voices
from that morning under the soon to topple towers,
where your ears may not.

I hear the medics
working frantically on the dying,
speaking softly to give them some hope,
so intent on prolonging life
they're oblivious to their own impending fate.

I hear the cops
barking orders, striving to move those
who were Lucky enough to be escaping,
then standing their ground in that thin, blue line
until there was no way out for them.

And I hear those Jakes,
selflessly saying, "let's do it."
As side by side, in the way they lived and died,
they climbed those staircases into memory.

Godspeed to them all, may we never forget
that it wasn't soldiers that day
but fathers and sons, wives and mothers,
who gave all for the American way.

10.11.01 Fliers
Catherine Sasanov

The dead wait for us
around every corner,

pressed against walls,

incessantly describing themselves
to anyone who will listen.

How long will it take them to disperse?

We're averting our eyes,
streaming into the earth—

whisked off then surfacing
miles from town

(the living move deeper down,
less confined than the dead).

It's not the smell of burnt metal
that blows into Brooklyn,

it's our cue
to open the photo album of disaster

over and over—
start the airplanes lodged in our heads.

Dust that clung to my friends,

Dust that wants to make ghosts
of the living,

I recognize you
from under the streetlights—

Canal Street and Houston—

The dead who insist
they aren't dead, only

missing—a word forming itself
in the long throats

of subways. You catch on our lips.
We don't know what we're saying.

So invoiced, rain-soaked, dog-eared, dirty.
We lay small fires at your feet.

Pauline Hebert, Monument Beach, Massachusetts, After Dark Coffee House, (Bagel Nook), 1998, Reading for Veteran's Day

Sugar from Heaven
Pauline Hebert

Arctic winds claw at the angel's wings.
Intent on her mission, she circles once, twice,
lands on the blue Honda,
deposits her whisper-light burden
on the engine block, still warm.
Smiling in satisfaction,
she flaps her wings, then is lost
in New England's first winter blizzard.

My boots shush through heavy snow.
I approach my Honda.
Sticky with half-frozen snow, my eyes tear
my heart, haunted decades ago
as I nursed casualties on a field of battle.

Tonight I've decided to finally re-join them.
I unlock the car door, remove a loaded .22 Beretta,
pocket the gun. I hear a peep then another,
follow the sound, open the hood,
retrieve a wet shaking fuzz ball,
tuck it under my coat
retrace my footsteps,
enter the cottage.

I move a rocking chair, closer
to a crackling wood stove
sit and cradle the tiny animal on my lap
shed my coat and boots.
"Before you left home you should've learnt
how to meow" I say softly,
place the handgun on the table
intention forgotten, rock the baby kitten,
name her "Sugar", tuck her under my chin.
I chuckle as I feel a wet nose, a warm tongue.

Long into the night we rock.
Eventually, we both sleep.
Every now and then
beneath the wings of angels
the soft kitten peeps.

Operation Lam Son 719
Gary Rafferty

Cocky, with pressed fatigues and shiny boots,
the ARVN elite- Rangers and Marines, pour into Laos.
Round the clock for three days,
in slat-sided cattle-trucks,
in night convoys with headlights ablaze.
In huge gaggles of Hueys,
while sleek gunships circle,
snap at the jungle like guard-dogs.
For 47 days at the Laos border we dance
to a chorus of incoming artillery, rockets and mortars.
Lines of choppers pass overhead,
an endless stream going and coming, night and day.
Heavy liftships return towing crippled Hueys
hung from nylon straps beneath their bellies.
We fire our cannons until the air shimmers like a
    mirage.
Fire until incoming shells blossom among us,
race our own ghosts to bunkers, and still it is not
    enough.

Over the radio we hear ARVNs
on firebases being swallowed whole.
Frantic words we don't understand
but the tone is the same in any language.
There's little water, food or hope,
hot steel the only thing plentiful.

Nixon on my transistor radio,
his voice distant and tinny,

like a message from the world
to a lost colony on another planet.
He proclaims 'victory on the plains of Laos'
the success of Vietnamization.'
The ARVNs trickle back in half a day.
Bandaged men who cling to dusty tanks
like flies to our corpses.

They pass our knocked-down, sandcastle firebase
possessed by the stare of men fleeing disaster.
They rush past a trailer by the edge of the road,
layered with bloated bodybags
all my friends in pieces.

Asian Pear
Preston H. Hood, III
(for Gary)

I watch him peel
the Asian pear
from the stem outward
so precise the downward spiral
of the paring—
that we pause.

He cuts slices for our mouths.

Some Are Rescued
"Elizabeth García"

The consul had said, don't touch her—
so they took my handcuffs off and not my hands.
I left on a plane with no door-gunner,
left behind
the blindfold, tanks, refugees,
mortars both imported and homemade,
the bodies they dismantled.

The consul had not saved my patients though,
had not put in that word.
I dreamed that they had saved themselves.

I returned to a place that was not home
and the words I knew:
capucha, cateo, yucca, caer
were homeless with me.
Therefore I could not name the knives that seemed to
       wait for me
every day in my kitchen
or the tone the hospital operator's voice
shared with the sergeant at the cell door.

Someone else must have told you
that by then I was afraid even of the knives implied
in the mountain ridge I knew as *sierra*.

The mail came one day, full of you,
what you'd written on torture and Franco,
what you'd written on surviving them.
I hid with your words under blankets
and wrote on your instructions.
I made myself write down what I knew
of the man who had lain
with his intravenous line slung from the crucifix,
two bloody limbs I repaired gloveless,
his mother near the market he thought still alive
and the worst fact, the not knowing,
if he'd crawled away or been taken.

I wrote down every face and betrayal
and slept then.
In the morning the mountains had reclaimed
    themselves
as mountains, the knife had gone
from the horizon.

It was not the words themselves that saved me
but wordless I would have died then.

Survival Tactics
Maureen Ryberg

Every hair on my head was a spike
piercing my skin. Fourteen days after
my first treatment I began to pull out
sheaves of it. My husband caught on camera
my eggshell fragility, and fear that made my pupils
black as tarns in an Icelandic night,
as if I had seen over his shoulder something

awful, out of darkness, hurtling. Oh,
what is hair (I sang), but a warm cover, a nest
for mice, or moles, or skylarks? Forget Samson—

strength is of the spirit (I told the face
steaming up the mirror). My tresses lay
in the sink, like hay, or angel pasta. Picture
the brain on chemotherapy: a tangled heap

of fishermen's nets on the floor of a shed,
coiled, like a cat-'o-nine-tails, ready to inflict
pain. Oh, what is suffering (I sang), but
purification? If we are singled out, allotted
sentences, a reckoning of days until harvest—
like peasants summoned by the bell in the hot fields
at high noon, we should bow down and close our eyes

(I whispered). (And I wept.)

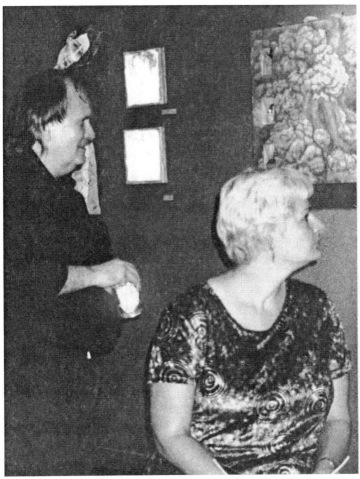

**Lyn Dorian and Fred Marchant, Boston, Massachusetts,
University of Massachusetts, Boston, Harbor Gallery, 2001**

Hair Pulling
Lyn Doiron

"Goodbye"
I mouthed the word.
The silver thread did not answer
but turned
and fell from fingers:
a stories-long descent
coming to rest
finally, in the pattern of the rug.

A moustache on the daisy
A glimmer on the floorboard
reunited with the others
woven into a nest of goodbye

And I, lover and the cause
of their demise (though they were dead
before we started),
grieve
when I sweep.

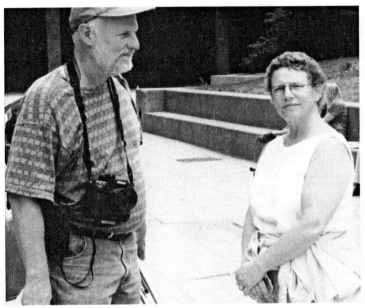

**Dianne Collins Ouellette and Doug Anderson, Boston,
Massachusetts, University of Massachusetts, Boston, 2001**

The Sheep of Umberleigh
Dianne Collins Ouellette

In Devon, we take our time among the sheep of
    Umberleigh.
Follow their droppings, walk in their mud tracks,
watch as they bleat and graze from one field to
    another.

At Tintagel, King Arthur's ruins, we master the steps
to the top of the cliff. The sun glories through the
    clouds
and I take off my hat, let the ancient wind bless my
    ravaged head.

The cliff, dotted with stones, marks rooms and
    weathered
remains. From the women's poetry area, I pick up
    pieces of slate,
sneak them in my pocket, hope to conjure magic.

I wonder what Guineverre prayed for—
words, harvest, Lancelot, babies.
I've had them all. What right do I have to complain?

On the way down the cliff, the sun plays through
clouds leaving ribbons of light. I hold these images:
lost sheep, Guineverre praying, God's spectacle.

In Backburn's Pub, the peat fire burns our eyes as we
   drink creamed tea.
In the distance, the remains of the castle, cliffed and
   wasted, fade.
Two weeks later, every sheep in Umberleigh will be
   dead—
burned in sacrificial piles.

Thoughts from a Green Armchair
Dorinda Foley Wegener

Leaving the constant flow of chores,
I have come from my house to his.
In father's green armchair—
I attempt solace.
He is at his desk, buried
by papers, photos of grandchildren.
Midday sun glints off a magazine
reflects on his platinum hair.
Outside, a grackle
lands on the patio, a ruffle
of iridescent wings—
a coarse call   unanswered.
See father's back turned, the blue of his shirt—
notice for the first time how it's fading.

Slouching Out Of Belfast, 1991
Edward Abrahamson

And what rough beast, its hour come round at last
Slouches towards Bethlehem to be born?
***The Second Coming**, W. B. Yeats, 1919*

The ferry leaves Larne and Ulster behind
on its daily round to Stranraer, Scotland
and vibrates into a calm North Channel
(the Northern Approaches convoy route
famous in two World Wars)
between Atlantic and Irish Sea.
Astern, in filtered morning sun
mist shrouded bluffs where hundreds
(or was it thousands?)

on the losing side, were squeezed over the edge
to the flaying surf on rocks below.

Was it two, or three hundred years ago?
Were they silent? Trembling in terror of heights?
Or did they bellow epithets against enemy, against tide
as earth above and sky below slowly traded place?
(It was a long way down.)

Were family groups dealt with together?
Did jeering victors offer those kinds of choices?
Did they bring *their* women and children
to celebrate these sacred rites?

I'll be asked about the Auld Sod
back in the states by Irish and Scots-Irish friends.
Dear friends, funny, earthy, generous friends.

But after the Green and the Orange
And the Red and the Black
And St. Andrew and St. Patrick
And St. George and St. Brendan
And the Book of Kells and the Union Jack
And the Protestant ministers and Papist priests
At thumping parades of bemedalled black suits
In the hail of stones, and rubber bullets and lead
In sweet smell of riot gas and blood-drenched remains
left in vengeance in charred rubble by masked gunmen
And pistols crackling at noisy para-military funerals
And the keening of widows in weeds
In the city that launched titanic

For the life of me
I can't make out which was the winning side.

And for all the written and oral tradition
And sodden toasts and Blarney tales
And sparkling Irish wit and dance
And passionate embrace
And poetry and prose, song and drama
The shimmering voices of joy and grief
And rags of starvation to exile

I can't remember which was the losing side.

Forgive me Irish Bard
an unlettered outsider traveling your Emerald Isle
born a few years before you passed on:

You spooked your present from a wobbly tower
with whimsy from the past.
Spouted splendid poetic thunder
though squirming athwart a prickly fence
feet tapping uncertainly to both sides.
No help really, no grand revelations
of any use to a traveling outsider.

Ah but your (1938) memoirs spoke to me so true:

*...We begin to live when we have conceived life
    as tragedy.*
...I think the common condition of our life is hatred.
*...One thing I did not foresee not having the courage
    of my*
own thought: the growing murderousness of the world.

Hear my tiny report oh Bard of Ireland, at Millenium's
End:

The issue was never in balance.
This murderous century's corpse twists in moan of
    random wind.
Each generation in your *gyres*
jealous of its signature
goose steps the elaborate script
into the same black pit.

Now my ship vibrates on its daily round to Stranraer
The salt air of a north wind chops the Irish Sea
A patient sun burns through mist.

Astern the cliffs at Larne.
I can't remember which was the losing side.
What can you expect from a traveling outsider
Slouching out of Belfast?

30th Anniversary of the Tet Offensive
Gary Rafferty

He settles in his seat like into a foxhole,
itching for a confrontation.
He's come in halfway through our reading,
half in the wrapper.
I know he's a vet by his eyes,
by the way he examines the carpet's weave,
as we spit out bullet-words, ambush-phrases.
Air-strike poetry, he can't help but understand.
I watch his eyes betray him, like body bags in war
they fill despite his every effort.

Afterwards he approaches, unsteady.
I can see the ghosts in his eyes,
jostling for space like commuters
on the 5 o'clock train out of South Station.
He tries to recite a practiced litany of units, tours.
But, memories overrun him, quick as N.V.A. regulars.
All he can do is squeeze of short bursts of words,
"First of the 27th... 25th Infantry... Started in '66..."
but he can't stay with it. His friend's faces waver
in the hollow glare of descending flares.
Pursued by legions only veterans see,
he branches off, first here, then there,
like the Ho Chi Minh trail weaves,
through the breathing jungle.
He repeats, "Four tours, FOUR TOURS!"
the way a fool speaks to the deaf,
convinced if he says it louder, we'll understand.

He flees to the student lounge, plops into an
    overstuffed sofa,
weary as he was his last day in-country.
"Why," he asks me, "why would anyone want to
    remember
something as horrible as Tet?"

Another time, I'd be brutal, ask him,
"Brother, has running from it worked for you?
We can't forget. Turn around. Face the ghosts.
Look them right in the eye."
But, I can't be cruel to him tonight.
Even if I said it, he'd only see
the movement of my lips,
every word drowned out
by the gunfire in his ears.

Yo Bruce
Preston Hood
(for Weigl)

we are just
passing through

like comets
burning out,
embers of firewood,

like a thread squeezed
through a needle's head,
eyes bulging

from kick ass
boyhood blow jobs
& freight train hopping poverty.

We remember
the crucifix, the crossing over,
the unattained love.

Yo Bruce,
we are just
passing through

from doing time
in Saigon
where the heart

is merchandise
sold on the black market
for firefights & rocket attacks.

Trickle down economics
like machine gunfire
rips through our backs—

the truest form
of self-deception—
fuckin' scary.

Yo Bruce,
we are just
thoughts

in the subconscious—
quiet flashes
where soldiers go to die.

Just passing through
from agent orange to acid rain,
the Birdland blues of discrimination,

steel mill slag blues of Lorain, Ohio
only to find *the strange unraveling*
back to every year's blues.

Passing through
to the youth we knew
but hoped to claim.

Is there time
for us to laugh more
than be angry,

love more
than be numb,
feel

we are not
someone
else's whore.

new moon
Steffanie Schwam

passion awakens
eggshells crack open
no I no you to grasp
both white and yolk quiver
then slide over

salmon thrash upstream
over rocky steps
no I no you to grasp
spawning ecstatic
dark moon and shudder

October's Toll
Jacqueline M. Loring

(for Chris)

He sits next to me,
his text book
the same
as mine.
I notice
the deep chocolate colors
of his cloak, his speckled gray hair,
his glance
back
over both shoulders.

During break in the back
corner
of the college class room,
he nods for permission
to speak,
asks me why children go out at night
dressed in hoods and masks,
and why Cambridge
people hang
sheets in trees.

E. B. Moore, Boston Massachusetts, University of Mass, Boston, 2001, Student reading at Joiner Center

When She Writes
E. B. Moore

(for Dianne Ouellette)

She peels herself—
an onion of torn skins
steeped like tea, the dregs

read and discarded,
their limp disguise unfit
for hiding. Her core free

unfolds in flowers she eats,
digests, and hawks back
to feed her selves—ferment

of selves fed and fed like clamorous
fledglings. She grows new,
a skin fit-out royal in feathers.

And dominion without end,
she flies—

**Gary Rafferty and Fred Marchant, Centerville, Mass. 2001,
Cape Cod Writers' Center, Summer conference**

You!
Gary Rafferty

The guys in Marine Recon adopted me. During my time off I'd hang around with these madmen and they humored my ignorance of all things Vietnam in a way I never could manage later. I never really understood why they liked me, usually Marines had scant use for `Doggies' which was their name for soldiers, but I wasn't one to question what I thought of as a good thing.

One day two of them, Whiley and Claymore walk up to me and asked if I'd care to go "outside the wire" with them. Well, I'm new in-country and the way they ask makes it clear this is more a dare, than an invitation. I look from one hard face to the other and not finding any room to squirm say, "Yes." You see the legends of my father and my uncles who'd all served in `The Big One' were still fresh in my head and well, I wanted some of that adventure.

I figure they meant sometime in the future but they mean, right now. So I half run back to my hooch and get my M-16, my claymore bag full of loaded magazines, my pistol belt with it's two canteens, my helmet and flack-jacket and I half-run back to them like some lost puppy and by God, if I had a tail I damn sure would be wagging it.

I meet them by their hooch and even I notice their faces have changed. They apply camouflage face paint in broad black and green stripes to my face and I'm glad they do cause my hands are shaking from the fear and anticipation of what I can't even imagine. They check me out, make sure my 16 isn't dirty and my canteens aren't half-full. They're not and I'm pleased to pass this small test from these men.

They put me at the end of their small file, where I realize later, I can do the least stupid things to endanger us all. We leave the wire by the side gate, lock and load, only half waking the MP slouched in his folding lawn chair in the afternoon sun. I'm very self-conscious in my plain OD fatigues next to their camouflage one's and I'm scared but, I place my feet carefully in the spots they've just placed their's and I manage to do this without falling flat on my face. The heat presses down on us like the flat iron my grandmother used when she pressed white sheets in the summer heat back home. By Christ, I'm sure wishing I was back there right now, but I'm more afraid of letting these men down than anything else.

We enter the tree line and into the sudden dark of the jungle slowly and carefully. I follow along trying not to crowd Whiley, yet still stay close enough to keep from getting lost out here. An upraised hand from Claymore in front halts us near a small clearing just ahead. There are lots of boulders here, it looks as if some giant has dropped them willy-nilly through the whole Que Son area.

I keep watch on a fan shaped area to each side and back the way we'd come, just as Whiley told me to before we left. I glance towards them and see Claymore making hand signals to Whiley, who comes back to where I crouch and he leans close as a lover and whispers, "Go right, 50 meters just past that clump of rocks and wait there, we'll come
and get you in a little while."

86

Well, now I'm really scared. I half figure they're going to leave me there, go back to base camp and have a good laugh with their Marine buddies about just how stupid doggies really are. But, I nod and I tell you my devotion to those maniacs was so strong if they had left me there, I'd still be there waiting for them to come back and get me. I go towards the clump of rocks, slow as molasses in a New Hampshire winter. Watch for snakes, trip wires and gooks with equal dread. I pause just before I go around the rocks because I think I hear something, but Christ the sweat is dripping down my face like a waterfall and as fast as I wipe it away it returns faster, so I'm not sure if I really heard something or if it's just the sound of my heart coming through my chest. I wait a while and not hearing anything, I step around that boulder, only to come face to face with an N.V.A. soldier.

Well, I don't know who's more surprised. But, my rifle is in my hand and his is leaning against the rock. In that elongated moment I see firmness in his eyes as he moves his hand toward his rifle. I'm so damn scared I pull the trigger back so hard the imprint of my finger is probably still in that steel receiver. I fire the whole magazine straight into his chest from no more than 8 feet away. Pieces of him fly out the back of his shirt in a spray made silent by the rapid chatter of the 16 in my ears. The Son-of-a-Bitch is dead on his feet, yet he walks towards me blowing red bubbles from his mouth and I swear they'd get as big as his head before they burst and as each of them bursts he says, "You!"

"You!" sprays onto my face with the force of slaps.

He steps right up to me as I fumble with the magazine release. As I try to get another magazine out of my claymore bag with my left hand, he reaches up and puts his small hand on my shoulder. Not hard but, exactly the way a friend holds you by the shoulder and as he bubbles one last,

"You!" he slides down the front of me, like I'd let the air out of him. The blood from his face and shattered chest leave a brush stroke of red down the front of me I never have gotten off.

After all these years, I'm still not sure if his voice has the tone of accusation or just surprise. Whether he's really saying the English word, `You' or some Vietnamese word that my terror transformed into, you. But, he returns to me every night in my sleep and he always says the same thing.

Section III.

…the road I walked in on
Preston H. Hood, III, *Against Idleness That's Encroaching*

A Community of Words, A Circle of Poets

Apogee
Dianne Collins Ouellette

Rocking in red chairs
we eat grilled salmon
and watch the storm
measuring the distance
against the echoing alleluias.

The children, wide eyed,
run in and out of the rain
trailing their laughter, their prayers.

That moment
between the lightning and thunder,
I live my life with you.

**Carmi Soifer and John Deane, Boston, Massachusetts,
University of Massachusetts, Boston, 2001**

Poet
for Tino Villanueva
Carmi Soifer

In my friend's story,
he is a migrant worker.
It is a true story.

He carries that small village of pain
over Texas ground
picking okra,

one generation removed
from the hurt
of cotton.

In town he is
pinned back against plyboard,
a laughed-at Chicano.

How did this man grow?
He will tell you:
I built myself

word by word
scaling language
like buildings,

rotating sounds
under my tongue
until

I could speak.

Words for You, Mother
Alice Barton

So now you have lost all of your nouns,
Not just the names of what, and where, and who you
    love.
You wander in thickets of verbs, adjectives, adverbs—
Of connectors that connect no thing, no one.

Your strong verbs—hope, love, dream, caress, pray
Worship, remember, sleep, eat, drink—
Lack the anchor of subject and object.
They want the people, places, and things you cannot
    name.

All right, then. I will follow you to the end
Carrying a heavy basket so full of nouns
It curves my back. I will hand you *rose, wine,*
God, book, poem, lily, sweet corn, child, husband.

I will give you *Dorothy Elizabeth, Edward David,*
    Alice Frances,
Priscilla Marie, Charlotte Anne, James Francis and
    Mary Margaret.
All sleep safely dreaming of *sheets* you have ironed
    smooth.
I give you also your beloved *Edward* now drinking
    from the *cup* of *joy.*

Karen D'Amato and Preston Hood, Boston, Massachusetts, University of Massachusetts, 2001

Full Light
Karen D'Amato

The light stole my best dress
What's left I take to the sea
so many grief's
the taste of salt and sour
hours spent mulling
what was said

how white petals of lisianthus
or my daughter's
breath at my breast
slip the edge
to where the present
never was

Happiness is etched
with a first husband's
life cut short
new fullness mine
though I lost him
and because

this naked overlay
of love

in the name of the surf skimming rock
in the light of the sun swimming shoulders
I shed and accept

Happiness
Thuy Dinh

My mother had told me that
to be beautiful means you can never be
comfortable.

I remember at four
rubbing my puffy skirt
fashioned out of wire and ruffles
against
skinny thighs dotted with mosquito bites.
(already, my feet, that year,
had outgrown the maryjanes.)

I remember at ten
peeling a guava
awkwardly and painstakingly
a left-hander grasping a dull peeler

I remember at fourteen craving
(having lived in America for one year),
Chinese water spinach and pickled eggplants,
fried tofu dipped in *nuoc mam* and,
"elephant mango" smeared with salt and red pepper—
(all to be eaten while squatting in my day-old
    pajamas.)

I remember knowing
that I would never be
beautiful or comfortable.

Victim's Name Unknown
Marcianne Lucia

I am on the floor of a subway car, my head to the
    ground
like everybody around me.   A huddled mass of
    humanity. This
is how fear acts. There are no distinctions between us,
all afraid.   Except for the boy who from above us,
    laughing
a little, tells us as though to chide, "Get up. It's over
    now."

A man, brown man in a baseball hat brim turned to the
    back,
is dead on the platform, sprawled where he fell.   It
    sounded like
a bottle rocket, less scary than a Chinese firecracker.
    A pop. Pop. Pop.
Sharp, but not too loud. Not loud enough to go down
    on your knees for
on the dirty floor of a subway car, your head bowed
    low.

A woman next to me says, "He is dead. I felt his
    pulse." Says it again.
And again. I felt his pulse. Like a prayer.   She
    clutches at her hands, presses them
to her heart. She could have been his grandmother.
    They are pumping at his chest
like on TV... A teenage girl to my left says, "Why you
    wanna go and watch them

save some dead boy?" to another. Yellow police tape
    ropes us in.

The cop, disgusted, spits at me, "What do you care
    about your train?
A person just died here." And he's right. They are
    letting us go, one
by one. Out into the night. Buses will arrive soon.
    Cameras watch us
smoking, talking, gesturing, walking away. Most of us
are black. The eyes of some of us are glazed.

Her voice is in my head. "I felt his pulse. He is dead."
    Pop.
Pop. Pop. Like a bottle rocket. We are on our knees.
Will this make the headlines tomorrow? Brown man
    on
a subway platform. "A person just died here."
I do not even know his name.

Pauline Hebert, David Connolly, Preston Hood, Jacqueline Loring, and Kevin Bowen, Boston Massachusetts, University of Massachusetts, 2000, *Moving Wall* Poetry reading

Summer Memory
Pauline Hebert

After the peace, after the broken
loves and failed career,
after the too many moves,
the too many hospitals, so sure
of their cures.
After the therapy, the falling naked
through the glass, after the therapy,
their long incantations into futility.
After the other man,
the thousand moments of rage
in his heart. After the ring,
the broken pacts, the lies
all around us like roaches,
we survive on the edge,
try somehow to live together.
My sister, brother climb
to the shuttered cottage
where I stay secluded.
I try to make them see
I can't be a lunatic
but here somehow
among the birds and trees,
the man's trapping strewn
indecently over the furniture
among the animals we answer to no one,
somehow here, with a future.
Today my brother pats my cheek
as if to re-live the past

the times I beat the odds
when the war had not intruded
in the black days of the 60's
and my sister hugs me,
all but an illusive hope
of recovery left
or no longer for me, that wish.

Poetry Reading, Jamaica Plain
Gary Rafferty
(for Do Chu)

Stand at this reading in the stifling heat
so far back I can't really hear.
The speaker's voices drift away,
wisps of words overwhelmed
by the tide of noise washing
in from the nearby street.
Half the poems are in Spanish
which I can't understand.
Kevin kindly motions for me to take his seat.
I sit beside Do Chu, a Vietnamese writer
who traveled here for the workshop.
He doesn't speak much English,
but he smiles at me.
We met earlier. He knows I'm a Vietnam Vet,
when and where I fought.
His grip is firm and the kindness
in his eyes is honest
and I have to question
if I could be so generous
were the situation reversed.
I barely understand one half of the words.
He understands none.
I imagine I'm in Hanoi listening to
Hmong or Lao poets in this same heat,
which there would be a balmy day.
I can't understand either of the languages
and am seated next to a former enemy.

Would I be as relaxed?
I watch him finger a plastic bag.
Slender fingers outline a razor.
I notice he needs a shave. So do I.
He takes the razor out of the bag
old style double edge kind
with a packet of extra blades.
I imagine its style is familiar.
It must be good to find something
familiar in a strange place.
Fingers move slowly along the outside
of the plastic molded over the handle,
anticipate it's feel, how it opens.
The sensation of it passing over a face.
The crispness of the air on our skin after.

David Connolly, Boston Massachusetts, University of Massachusetts, 2000, Reading from Anthologies, *From Both Sides Now* **and** *Writing Between the Lines* **at Joiner Center**

To The Vietnamese Veterans
Dave Connolly

I've wanted to tell you all,
as I've met each of you over the years,
"Tôi mang dâú dau thúóng cho Vietnam."
I bear the mark of pain for Vietnam.

No matter which side you were on,
the war has cost me; it is long over for me.
I hope it is over for you,
especially if it was between us.

But is what I have said the truth?
For what do I bear that mark?
Did I almost fall for your homeland,
or for mine?

Was it that challenge to "Ask not,"
and Kennedy's Camelot?
Was it for me, my father, or yours,
for Southie, the States, or Saigon?

See, all of you,
on both sides, can know and say
for what it was you dared,
maybe almost died.

And all of you,
can say you fought for,
bear the mark of pain for,
your country, for Vietnam.

I fought for something,
something I cannot yet name.
That is the truth,
and the problem.

After the War
Dorinda Foley Wegener

John lives on
a mountain haloed by sky.
He has a flag.

He has a past.
A memory with secrets
worse than any head wound.

Look at his feet.
One is crooked.
Look back

to his face
his mountain
his flag, burning.

**Vasco Pires, Falmouth, Massachusetts, 2000, 1st Annual
Katherine Lee Bates Poetry Festival**

Montgomery To Memphis
Vasco Pires

Way down in the State of Alabama, USA
I went to visit a church one day.
A church on Dexter Avenue where Martin Luther King
once spoke with pride.
White painted stairs rising on either side,
up to an entrance leading to a hall inside.
Dr. King talked of civil rights,
and new dreams coming our way.
It all started one December day,
when a tired Black woman refused
to give her seat away.
Rosa Parks had worked all day in a dusty mill.
She only wanted to get home and chill.
Rosa sat in the first seat she found on the bus.
A White man started a fuss.
"Nigra, you can't sit with us."
There was a law, they say,
that this seat was not for her on any day.
He hemmed and he hawed,
and the police, they did call.
Rosa, they said, you must move back.
Give that man this seat.
She replied, "No, sir!
I have been working all day

in a dusty old mill,
and my feet are hurting me still.
I will stay in this seat,
because I am tired and beat.
No sir, I will not give up
this seat today."

Engine 8; 27 Burke Street; Medical Emergency
Gary Rafferty

They said he was sitting in the wood rocker smoking
his pipe.
Chilled, he wore his wife's fleece bathrobe,
he coughed and embers fell in his lap.

Greedy yellow flames pulsed, then flared.
He stood, ran in a tight terrified circle.
When we arrive;

the old man stands,
hairless as a newborn,
in the middle of the room.

Only clothing spared by flame,
a BVD waistband.
Huge blisters sag from his arms

opaque vestments of agony.
He keeps his arms outstretched
pleading for supplication.

By reflex I lower my eyes, pray; *God, have Mercy.*
When I raise them,
he looks so tiny,

collapsed in on himself,
surrounded by an oval of ash,
like a white dwarf star.

We spread the shock-yellow burn sheet
out on the floor, have him step onto it.
Gently dribble sterile water over him,

try not to calculate the pain of each drop.
Through a split in the slough of his face, he says,
"Oh, boys, that feels good."

Uniforms
Jacqueline M. Loring

It was summer, Miss Vanasse and I had just finished a delivery with Dr. Leonard Smith. After I wheeled the baby to the nursery and the mother to the post partum floor, I began to wash down the labor room. Miss Vanasse was busy washing the delivery instruments for me to wrap and autoclave when the Delivery Room desk phone rang. I watched the look on her face change and I knew it was the Director of Nurses on the phone. Miss Vanasse turned to me and said that I was to report to the X-Ray Department. A Kennedy had broken a leg and the President's wife was on her way to the hospital. I didn't move.

"Miss Barton said immediately," I remember Miss Vanasse saying to my unbelieving, stone face. Miss Barton's "immediately" meant just that so I grabbed a drab green, cloth coat from the wooden hook outside the Doctor's Lounge to cover my delivery scrub outfit consisting of pants and a shirt. Due to the fact that I am six feet tall Miss Vanasse had allowed me to wear doctor's pants instead of the knee length scrub dress that delivery room and operating room nurses wore. I put my arms through and tied it in the back as I walked the couple of steps to the elevator outside the delivery room door. The knot of my cloth cap and the tie to the white cloth mask tangled in back of my neck and I wrestled with them as I turned the corner at the elevators and opened the door to the staircase between the nursery corridor and 2nd Main. I took the metal stairs two at a time, down past the first floor to the basement and opened the door outside the pharmacy. I remember breathing hard as I strode past the left hallway to the Emergency Room, past the first x-ray rooms. Tom, the Chief X-ray Technologist, was standing in the hall speaking to a tanned woman in shorts and a scarf. We all had our jobs. I headed for the stairway at the end of the hall, past X-ray. As I opened the stairwell door, someone brushed by me. In a moment I can see and feel and hear to this day, my whole world stopped for a heartbeat. There about to take the last stair, her eyes riveted on the door and on me, was the most beautiful woman I had ever seen. I say beautiful because if you need me to describe her and that moment in one word, it is all I have to describe Jacqueline Kennedy. I also cannot tell you in one or two words what I really mean by beautiful. I can only describe the moment by telling you that in front of me was a tall, thin, tanned woman in shorts and a bandana holding back her hair. Her bangs fluffed on her forehead as she took the last step.

I have only told this story a couple of times. My friends want me to describe Mrs. Kennedy and so I begin with the set of her jaw, the concern in her eyes. It is a more simple truth than what really happened.

Remember I knew that Mrs. Kennedy would be in the stairway and with every step from the delivery room to the x-ray department, I knew I would see her for the first time, be in the same place as Jacqueline Kennedy. What really happened is a bit embarrassing. I opened the door, as I said and as she put her foot on that last stair she look directly at me. To this day I cherish that look because it was a look of trust, of honesty, a look to me. And what did I do? For that

116

heartbeat, I expected to hear trumpets. Crazy but even today as I write about what did happen in that stairway I expect to hear sound because inside my head trumpets were saluting her. But of course, there were no trumpets. When our eyes met, in that skip of my heart, I bowed my head as if I was saying the Hail Mary and came to the part about "blessed is the fruit of thy womb, Jesus…" At least I didn't genuflect. When my head came up from my bow, she was standing there. "Miss Barton sent me," I managed to stammer. Now, today, I know how lucky I was to have found those words. For without the where-with-all to get those four words out of my mouth, I know I would have been one with the plaster on the stairway wall as the other men in back of Mrs. Kennedy poured down the stairs to crowd in back of her as she paused in front of me. A big, very square man in a dark suit, taller than my six feet, was holding the door open in back of me. He let Mrs. Kennedy walk through the door and then me. I took three or four steps and pointed out for her the small office between the x-ray rooms where I had seen Tom escort the other woman who turned out to be Joan Kennedy. Suddenly the tight x-ray corridor was filled with people I didn't recognize. A small child lay on the x-ray table in the room to the left of the office being comforted by the two women. I stood outside watching inconspicuously, waiting to be needed.

I saw Miss Barton before she saw me. She turned the corner from the ER and made her way through the crowd who initially had their backs to her. It seemed to me that once she saw the people in the hallway her mood turned. It was a change I had learned to anticipate during the 18 months I lived in the student nurse's dorm and was lucky enough to have the Director of Nurses who happened to be the Director of the School of Nursing living next door to me. I was instantly sorry for the secret service person about to get to know that look.

Past everyone, Miss Barton strode, her uniform swishing in the silence that accompanied her arrival. She stopped directly in front of me.

"Miss Murray?" she said. I had also learned as a student that there was no answer to that question. I had somehow found the words for Jacqueline Kennedy but for Miss Barton there was only a dry throat and nausea rising from my instantly, tightly knotted stomach. She said nothing else. Her back was to everyone but me so no one ever knew what happened next. The look on her face was somewhere between rage and disappointment. She looked me squarely in the eye as she said my name, her hands moved to her hips. Her eyes told me that I had committed a terrible sin, a sin against one of her unforgivable commandant. I was not in uniform.

The ankle was diagnosed as sprained, crutches and meds prescribed and the press arrived all without me being present, not this time anyway. I was back in Labor and Delivery waiting for Miss Barton. This was not the last time I ran to her call to escort a prominent patient or to wind the way through the medical maze for a famous family or to sit with a dying patient. There would be other adventures but it was the only time I ever arrived at an event not wearing my nurse's uniform perfectly starched and pressed. I had learned that day a lesson I should have known. In the future, when I presented myself as a Licensed Practical Nurse, a graduate of Miss Barton's School of Nursing, I would proudly wear my clean, crisp, white cap with its light blue, velvet ribbons up the side and it would sit exactly on the top and back of my head.

I remember to this day the deep brown eyes of Jacqueline Kennedy meeting mine in trust. It was an enormous personal moment for me. I also know that waiting for Miss Barton in the Labor Room that afternoon, all I could think of was that I would have missed the moment with Mrs. Kennedy in order not to have disappointed Miss Barton.

Recurrent Nightmare
Pauline Hebert

As the day winds its way to sundown
when the stars and the moon appear
you come to me in green fatigues
nameless, vague faces
with eyes of condemnation.
You need extract a price
unknown to me
one I cannot fathom
one you will not share with me.
How can I redeem myself
surviving when you died?
How could miracles save you
with brain cells scattered
amid the muck, blood,
bone of your shattered skulls.
I was no warrior.
I never shot, searched and destroyed
but I was witness to the abominations,
becoming a pacifist
in the midst of war.

**Maureen Ryberg and John Deane, Boston, Massachusetts,
University of Massachusetts**

SUMMER CARAVAN
Maureen Ryberg

In slow motion they move
camel-happy across the morning
towards the singing sea,

loaded down with instruments
of pleasure: towel, cooler, chair, umbrella.
One man stands, spread-eagled, bare

but for a sarong of geometric cotton
below his bulging midriff.
He reaches out, as if beseeching

some higher power to interfere.
One old lady holds a parasol
at ceremonial height, loving

its shade. Already, it is fire hot.
The first man turns his back to the sun,
enduring more, begging for more. Beyond

the pulsing of the waves, the soporific
hum of the eternal, a bearded man
combs the beach with a metal detector

and a nondescript woman
sits on the sea wall, rapidly
moving her pen across paper.

**Preston Hood & Michael Casey, Boston, Massachusetts,
University of Massachusetts, 2000**

Against Idleness That's Encroaching
Preston H. Hood, III

Like an autumnal leaf, I'm combustible.
I tremble to think that the dark
inclination of Nam rage
still lurks beneath. Just now,

I loose the patience of the bird watcher
adjusting the focus of the binoculars,
looking through them, I realize
fifty years of my life are over.

How sad each year seeing less,
feeling the cold more,
such unspeakable darkness.

There is no reconciliation
for forgetting the road I walked in on.

Beyond myself
the crimson marigold sun
lifts me.

Leaning over the balcony
I watch five chickadees dart into a tree.

If for a second I turn away,
they may be gone.

When my memories return to heartache
light gives way to dark
& nothing holds me to this world or the next.

A Communication from my Grandmother
Sarah Furo

The light went out of me.

Three small children,
this time my own babes
could not tie me to this life.

On a hot day in July
I walked into the river
behind the asylum
and it cooled me so.
I could think of pleasure
for the first time since
the sorrow of my beloved's death
had wrung me dry.
And I never walked out.
My dress heavy, my steps
slower and deeper until
I was gone into the wet
place from where I came.

My thoughts, my face
my duty to family
erased in water.

In a police rampage
my beloved was beaten down
and carried home to die
in front of me and our children.

I had already raised
ten brothers and sisters,
carried from Europe
by my mother's desire
for us to learn.
I went first, a scholar
in places no women
were allowed to enter.
I withstood the disdain
of those very halls where
the truth is sacred.
Small and serious
my destiny was clear.

And then I met my love.
From that day I was a bird
in flight with another,
my work and his entwined.
Who may judge me, if I
followed his departure
with my own?

**Dianne Ouellette, Franconia, New Hampshire, 2000, AMMI
Collaborative Poetry Workshop**

When I Come Back
Dianne Collins Ouellette

Dragonflies have the right idea.
Fluttering, shimmying,
elegant in their
blue wings that catch a
whoosh
of air.

They make love while flying,
eat while
soaring,
land just long enough
to catch
their breath.

Section IV.

...in the earth forever time
Preston H. Hood, III, *What Comes Next*

Swan Dive
Pauline Hebert

In need of a new "therapist", I enter a farmhouse
sadly in need of paint. I notice a sign labeled:
   "Prosper".
that alone should have warned me off.
A woman introduces herself,
stringy gray hair hangs in her face.
She wears a granny dress in need of a dye job,
at least an introduction to an iron.
I give her a thirty year synopsis, how my life
has been dragged through a dumpster
after a year in Vietnam as an Army Nurse.
She interrupts: "After ALL your years in therapy…
I can't believe…no one ever taught you
to breathe…" In hand she has Glamour magazine.
"…they have this terrific article on post traumatic
   stress."

In my mind's eye, I picture both of us
on the roof of the Empire State Building.
I calmly back up to the very edge of the roof
extend both arms from my side, shoulder height,
bounce once, twice. She says: "Of course,
the trauma they discuss
is from car accidents…but the principles are the
   same…"

I launch myself upwards, concentrate on the five
and a half somersaults in the pike position I've got to
    do
before I begin my swan dive.

"You'll need group work…" she chortles
"as well as one-on-one therapy with me…"
I begin my free fall. Windows flash by.

"I can cure you…" she cries leans over the parapet
as I recover from a double helicopter twist.
I am already in a tuck position, well on my way
past the twentieth floor when it occurs to me
that murder might be a more viable option.
I see myself, Uzi in hand, blast her,
all her Salvation Army refugee furniture,
into oblivion.   She shrieks: "…as for your panic
    attacks,
you'll have to give up caffeine…"
My body hits the pavement, does a dead cat bounce.
I'm jolted awake. But I still can't explain why
I am clutching the latest issue of Glamour magazine.

The Keeper
MaryEdna Salvi

Then shut up the asylum
and walk towards the heat
of the sun.

the outstretched hand
with crusted palm
and no life line…

the bruised face
that once
you thought you loved…

the swollen stomach
filled with
the pain of hunger…

will not follow you
all is silent now
(the key burns in your pocket)

**David Connolly, Sanford, Maine, 2000, Sanford Vets Center,
Veteran's Day reading**

Come On Home
Dave Connolly

"A rucksack is the backpack that infantrymen live
out of. In this song lyric, it is used a symbol for all of
the destructive baggage that too many Vietnam
Veterans still carry from that war and have yet to work
through."

Sometimes I think about good friends
and how it was that they met their ends,
boys who knew about thick and thin
and the shape that left my head in.
Hey, no matter what it was you did,
you were just a little kid.
and what you did or you didn't do,
we can work that through.

Try remembering those brave young boys,
the desperate times and the dangerous toys,
how they lived and how they died,
you know they're still right by your side?
Try thinking what they might do,
if they were still alive like you.
And that old rucksack you've been leaning on?
Pick it up. Put it on.

It was oh, so long ago and oh, so far away,
but for those who chose to go, it still seems like
yesterday.

Yeah, I remember my old Bros
and no matter how my life goes,
I throw my shoulders back because I know
who it is and what I owe.
I think of what they could have been
and I've got to make my life mean
something more for those souls who
died for me and you.

Don't forget about what it cost,
nothing won and so much lost.
No matter what, if you did your part
don't let that damn war claim your heart.
Stand your ground, Brother; can't you see,
those boys died for you and me?
So that old rucksack you've been leaning on?
Pick it up and put it on.

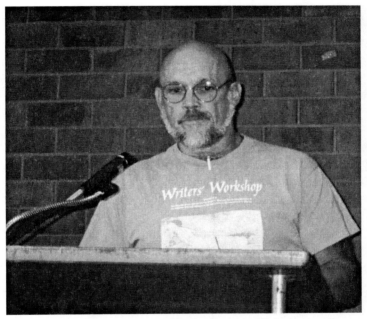

**Preston Hood, Boston, Massachusetts, University of
Massachusetts, 2000, Student reading at Joiner Center**

Tryptich: The Devil & the Fossil
Preston H. Hood, III

"Becoming is Rarely Pretty": a sculpture by Lynn
   Doiron

i.
Blood like cool aid forms the Devil.
A mothball plastered design—
the double vision
of cross-eyed rosettes
inside.

ii.
In a culvert beneath a road
spiders & snakes crawl over me.
I'm five, afraid
I won't make it to the other side.
Why did I crawl in here
miles from home?

iii.
I'm six, she is five.
"Drop your pants," I say.
I pull off mine

I touch her vagina,
she touches my penis.

She tells her parents.
Our parents don't talk to each other
anymore.

How To Cry
Gary Rafferty

(to friends at the William Joiner Writer's Workshop)

Three hours sleep tonight.
Like a kid the night before the first day of school.
I look forward to seeing old friends.
You'd think after years I'd relax- but to enter the
    writer's zone,
I must enter the Militarized Zone.
Conscious or unconscious I recreate it all.
Today I got my hair cut. Short.

The tiredness that sucks the marrow
from my bones returns on day two.
I've learned to recognize the journey
to my place of writing.
A return to some bachelor's bunker
where there's plenty of room and
a favorite leather chair
who's folds remember mine.
But there's something about the place
and the dreams that infiltrate my nights
which makes me eager to leave.

My body remembers, trauma spreads cell to cell.
Now comes a reluctance to shave and bathe.
Went forty-seven days without a shower there.
Water and hope equally scarce.
Before you wrinkle your nose in disgust,
believe me it was nothing
compared to the smell of death.

People, even writers who should know better,
ask why I most always write about the War.
My fingers are rebellious,
my brain's a bad influence on them.
By day three a rawness appears,
can't sleep, don't care!
Tears and words flow freely.
My digits dance across the keys like
bullets stitched across dusty earth.
I write what I must. I'm still practicing.
Took me 30 years to remember how to cry.
It's not good to forget some things,
impossible to forget others.

Building a Raft at the Pond
Dave Connolly

My neighbors at the pond thank me
for what they think is "hard work,"
four hours under a clear, July sky,
cold beers and easy laughs
over the screw-ups we each made
(and didn't want the wives to see,)
working with two upright men, fathers,
who come home from a day's work in the sun
and throw their kids in the pond.

"Hard work?"

All I could think of was the Nam,
digging and building defensive positions,
using whatever we had or could find each night,
working to put something, anything between us
and the Viet Cong rockets and mortars;
see, they always knew where we were.

So this here raft isn't work; it's pure joy.
I don't think I'll tell my neighbors why;
they wouldn't understand.

But I'll damn sure tell their sons.

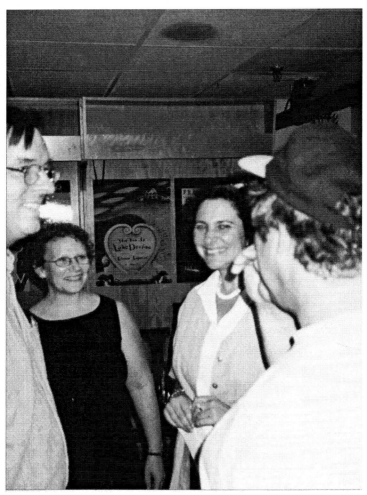

**Steffanie Schwam, Dianne Ouellette, Gary Rafferty, and
David Green, Brookline, Massachusetts, Brookline
Booksmith, 2001, Reading at Night of Women Readers**

hunger
Steffanie Schwam

drives me to till
the soil of my flesh.

fingers plow straight furrows
in my arms and chest.

blood seeps into the fluted soil,
prepares it for seeding.

if I make the soil ready,
will you come?

Oak Leaf and Acorn
Sarah Furo

Imagine, the Lady Oak Leaf,
slim profile turned
'til she is a single line, visible,
only in the maracas she grips
in delicate brown hands.

Shake, shake the noisy gourds—
she compels the spirits to gather.

Meanwhile,
Lord Acorn forces a stunning
whistle through the hole at the top
of his scaly beret,
shrill cry of a hawk as it circles
under the sun's beams.
The sound pierces the fog,
directs the action.

Aligned with the sound
of drums and flutes,
I plunge into the shake, shake,
like a pilgrim who wades
a holy river, worn with use.
The sound around no longer
the sharp scream
of the of the acorn cap
nor the wet sound of moving water,
but smoky and dark,
and I am a bird lost over

the ashen remains
of a burnt out forest.

When I find my way through
the smoke and gently floating ash,
I emerge into silver water,
this time the real thing
and I am salmon, a silver
crescent leaping in moonlight.

Lady Leaf wraps her arms
around my fish body,
while I lie on the wooden planks,
of the pier where I have been
summoned by the Moon's purpose,
supported by Lord Oak.
I smell the sweet joy of water,
but feel the charge of flip, flop,
snaking power through my spine.
Washed and cleansed by sound,
I open my mouth wide
my round fish mouth searching
for breath, and pull in death,
experience breath as tide,
the tide of spirit thrives,
a replacement for the solid waste
of regret and denial.

All of this took place on Wednesday.
The next Friday night
I had seen enough of my new clothes
to know I was unsealed,
uncorked and shimmery

an oyster hoisted from its shell.

I filled the bathtub
with lukewarm water and salt
and set myself to soak
in the sea of unshed tears.

Lady Oak Leaf wrapped me in a sheet
of soft breathing silk: wood smoke.
Held in her smooth embrace
I can still feel the veined walls of her arms.

Lord Acorn stood guard over my dreams.

Two Voices
Cornelia Veenendaal

Walking home from the station,
I hear behind me the voices
of a girl and boy.

"Some evenings I log on and work
till I'm wiped out. I think
it must be midnight. It's only 8:30!"

"I like to greet the dawn
with my favorite computer game,
Dr. Diavolo."

A slight sound of scraping,
like a pulled suitcase,
keeps step with them.

"I hate to wake up at dawn," she says.
"I do anything I can to keep
from waking up at dawn—

the birds are so loud."
In my mind's eye, the first light
seeps through dark leaves.

And when I finally turn
I see them, arm in arm,
her white cane brailing the way.

Imagine: cotton sheet at her ear
folds and whispers, as once
the fibers spoke in the wind.

The dazzle of leaf tap
on the window screen,
steps of the cat across the floor,

light crossing the floor
as it rises in leaves
with no more sound than leaven.

Comfort Food
Thuy Dinh

I chose the path of parenthood in the same manner that I became a refugee, a sudden trajectory into the unknown, a reckless leap of faith. Labor pains at thirty-six were as awful and scary as the sudden lift-off in a military aircraft at thirteen, the mind thinking that the body was poised at the precipice, ready for a free fall.

This terror of the unknown somehow metamorphosed into an obsession with food and cooking. I began to be preoccupied with providing food for Aline soon after she was born. During the days when I was still nursing my daughter, I gave her formula bottles to supplement her diet, not confident that my breast milk was sufficient. I did not enjoy the nursing process, feeling helpless that my young daughter was so dependent on my body for her sustenance. I clung to my orderly mind, dismissing a body that tried to recover from a difficult childbirth, a body burdened with changes, like a teeming Vietnamese forest, like a lumbering flat footed animal, like a punishing mystery. I resented the aftermath of my fertility. I yearned for aridity and thinness, the manifest destiny of a floating world free from all physical flaws. After the euphoria induced by pregnancy, the hormone depleted post-partum period literally represents a woman's fall from grace. I became depressed and confused, living between the past and the future.

151

In my usual neurotic way, I tried to control destiny with the act of preparing food for my young daughter. Soon after she cut her first teeth, I bought the best organic foods and cooked an endless array of gourmet meals for her—pasta simmered in home-made, free-range chicken broth; organic asparagus sautéed with cream butter and garlic; parmesan reggiano cheese and fuji apples; whole milk yogurt prepared with fresh seasonal fruits. I did not consult cookbooks, but simply started cooking, driven partly by memory, partly by instinct. My cooking for Aline transubstantiated my hang-ups into expectations for my young daughter: that she will grow big, strong and confident; that she will excel in competitive sports; that she will be worldly and incisive; that she will reject all the junk and noise of pop culture; that she will belong and dominate.

In the early days when my family first arrived in this country, I remember my mother and grandmother spending countless hours preparing meals for my father and grandfather, who had to work the afternoon-to-midnight shift in a parking garage. I remember watching them cook, and longing for the sweet, nutty taste of the home fried potatoes, or a morsel of the leanest, most tender steaks that were reserved for my father and grandfather. We the children had to make do with much less. But it was taboo to talk about food, as it was taboo then to talk about our reduced circumstances. It was beneath our dignity. My mother and grandmother poured their love and hopes into the food they prepared for their husbands, as if to remind my father and grandfather that they were still well-cared for, despite the menial jobs they had to accept to support our family and our refugee status. From that time on, I have always associated the all consuming act of food preparation as an unconscious manifestation of an inferiority complex.

I realize that cooking has given me another self: the self of an artist wanna-be, the self of a free spirit that rejects history and ethnic origins. I sing of upscale organic food, of pretty, polished yuppie food that has no visible subtext, no inner chaos. Yet, at the same time, I am never free from the lures of my childhood's comfort food. Comfort food, like Homer's sirens, steers you toward the rocky and turbid river of your past. When I feel nostalgic, I talk to friends about the food I grew up with: cow's kidney soup with chives— the Vietnamese equivalent of chicken soup—good to have when I was sick; rice porridge cooked with pig's blood and eaten with fried dough was an ideal, protein-rich breakfast; greasy egg rolls filled with crabmeat, accompanied by sea abalone soup that was garnished with the spongy lining of a pig's stomach, were festive staples for the death anniversary of an elder relative; sticky, resinous tropical fruits like milkwood and mangosteen bring to mind hot summer days lazing on the front stoop, sucking on the pungent fruits and smelling the impending monsoon.

I don't feed my daughter any of the comfort food of my past. Comfort food leaves you at the margin of culture. Comfort foods remind me of the stench and mud of Chinatown, or the open markets in Vietnam. Comfort foods evoke images of dark refugees shuffling along dangerous urban streets, their lives stunted by the misfortune of their late arrival. Comfort foods yield smells that cling to your hair and clothes. True comfort food is often salty and greasy—a high risk to your health. Comfort food represents the precarious border between acceptance and taboo, like a lover's slightly peculiar but charming sexual hang-ups. I am often repelled by my Asian girlfriends' passion for sucking marrow off chicken bones and the crunching noise they made when they gnawed on the brittle bones.

You can tell your child so much about your past, or nothing at all. Sometimes I wonder if too much knowledge about a parent's past will make her feel different, confused and afraid. Comfort food, the dramatic and scary stories of my childhood—these are elements of a chaotic universe from which I want to protect my daughter, yet I also realize that my hopes for her future and my belief in her American destiny represent as much an illusion as my parents and grandparents' attachment to the past.

Aline, now nearly four, is completely oblivious to all the baggage that I attach to food and cooking. There are days when she prefers McDonald's to my gourmet neuroses. I hope that she will grow up to be wise. I hope that she will always be happy. I hope that she will continue to be transformed by adventure and not be warped by pride or prejudice. As to the rest— my refugee's past, the future—these things will somehow work themselves out in due time. In the mean time, I have to wrestle with irony, self-doubts and great expectations—for without this struggle, I would not be able to tell the story of how I became a citizen of the United States.

Da
Preston H. Hood, III

(for David Connolly)

He likes the sky.
He likes the beach.
His kids love him, write
poetry about him, his wife
Lisa loves him, helps him
to direct his combat arrows
of grief into powerful words,
his new son Jake loves him
is now the Pokemon he needed to be,
trading his cards for dreams
his Da once stole from the dark.
Love for his family, his friends
has been his Irish greatness.
The work of building a raft
at the pond with friends
makes it all worthwhile.
'Someday' is always now with David.
The present had years to find him,
the war too silent
much too silent to explain.
We all love him,
with his wind harp pick
of Irish songs from the pub.
We love him because
in his heart we are just right.

Martha's Vineyard Bonito
Gary Rafferty

> *"The rest of the world was nowhere... Just nowhere.*
> *Gone, disappeared; swept off without leaving a*
> *whisper or a shadow behind."*
> Heart of Darkness, Joseph Conrad

Everything's a smudge of fog
except a puddle of sea around us.
The clumsy sun probes down,
forces patches of yellow tint,
as sudden bonito break water around us.

Another boat, The Lorelei, floats in from nowhere.
Her first-mate's reel sounds a painful howl,
and there, just there, offered up
in a big swell that rises between us,
the hooked bonito races
inches blow the surface.
Illuminated by a spotlight of sun behind us,
every scale reflects blue-green-amberlight.
As this underwater meteor
splits the sea.

The tension snaps with his line.

156

Vision, Ghost Ranch, 1998
Jacqueline M. Loring

With the Magpie, they soar
Kitchen Mesa, sweep down
Chimney Rock, spread their wings
across
the high-desert valley,
rustle Cottonwoods,
leave feathers for dreamers,
whisper, capture me,
capture me.

Mary to Her Brother
Dorinda Foley Wegener

Lazarus,
I prayed all psalms and songs
at my narrow window, my God's eye.
Brother,
I crept slowly down
watched in magical fear.

Lazarus,
last night I spied—
they removed your napkin and graveclothes.
Brother,
I remember each disciple,
where they placed their hands upon you.

Lazarus,
you woke to my singing,
now we are both adherent.
A miracle, a parable.
You whispered and we kissed—
the kiss of the Lamb.

When All This is Over
Dianne Ouellette

When all this is over, I mean to
stamp in puddles so that
it splashes up under my dress
wetting my panties, making them cling
in ways I've forgotten.

When all this is over, I mean to
hold babies not my own,
then give them back to their mothers'
when I've had enough.

When all this is over, I mean to
have a party, dance the tarantella
the hokey-pokey, the mashed potato
and get funky with jive,
as soon as I have the energy.

When all this is over, I mean to
make up for the bitchy days,
the crabby ways,
the downright shit that I was.

When all this is over, I mean to
go fishing with my Dad,
hang my feet in the water, go
overboard, remember when
the blues were running.

When all this is over,
I mean really over,
I'll see where the white boat waits.

What Comes Next
Preston H. Hood, III

We find the end by mixing tears with happiness
burning with the agony of how much war consumes
knowing no love or god or spirit can claim us
by revisiting all the paths walked, all the darkness
we traveled, the sorrow in the mouth deep love we lived.
We find the constellations of our lives by dismantling the
      pain
of the body, enduring the past of our delinquencies,
while recovering the lost youth stripped from us.

& in the earth forever time we see life for what it is:
a hand that leads us, unrecoverably into sorrow;
here, we desperately insist on passion
wandering among the dead of us, within
the old shells of our bodies wondering whether
something laughable or peaceful or real comes next.

Cape Cod Massachusetts, Summer Home

Contributors

Edward Abrahamson began committing poetry and other forms of writing later in life because, as he put it, he needed to "collect the material first." Born in Czechoslovakia, he emigrated to America during World War II and later served in the 101st Airborne Division. Fascination with people and history, dead or alive, is reflected in his work. He is in his second year of proving that "life is viable without a car even living in the suburbs…well most of the time." His preferred means of transportation now is bicycle, though he is a licensed pilot and was on occasion pressed into the crew of a friend's yawl. In the last decade he has cycled through eleven countries in his quest for new material with a notion that he'll have "more time to write" when eventually he pilots a wheelchair. He has published and presented professional papers in engineering and technical journals, written limericks for a cycling newsletter and was president of a children's advocacy organization.

On poetry and the writing community:

The Joiner Center experience opened my eyes to a wider world of poets, writers and damn fine people, many of them veterans, with deep and broad life experiences. Interaction and constructive critique with other students and world-class faculty was energizing. It stimulated writing in directions that I hadn't considered before.

Alice Barton - From my earliest years, I always wrote about things that delighted or bothered me. Even though I loved poetry and had taught it for years, I never thought about actually writing a poem until I went to my first poetry reading at Mount Holyoke several years ago. I heard Stephen Spender read, and I was overwhelmed. During the next weeks, almost in spite of myself, I wrote my first poem. The poem, addressed to "Spender", almost deified him. But at that reading I came to realize that "people", not specially anointed "poets" wrote poetry. I continued to write poems for some years after that, but I didn't consider myself a poet, and I showed my poems to very few people. My first attempt to read my work in a writing group in Boston failed. A friend had to read my poems for me. The affirmation that I got from that group helped me to begin to think of myself as a poet and to start trying to get published. I have continued to work with that Boston group and with another on Cape Cod where I live. I have attended workshops in Truro and Provincetown. By far my most intense and rewarding experience of working with writers was at the Joiner Center Writing Conferences at U/Mass Boston. I have won a few local awards and have been modestly published both locally and nationally.

Dave Connolly served as an infantryman with the 11th Armored Cavalry Regiment and is a proud member of Vietnam Veterans Against the War. He is one of the founders and original board members of the Joiner Center and holds a BA in English from UMASS/Boston. Dave is the poetry editor of The South Boston Literary Gazette and the author of the prose and poetry collection, "Lost In America." He lives in Southie with his wife, Lisa and his son, Jake.

Karen D'Amato is a Boston poet who teaches poetry, writing and English composition at Curry College in Milton and conducts poetry workshops in greater Boston public schools. Her poems have been published in a number of anthologies, including *Grolier Prize 1998* and *When a Lifemate Dies: Stories of Love, Loss and Healing.* She lives in Jamaica Plain with her husband and five-year old daughter.

Thuy Dinh is a writer and attorney living in the Washington, D.C. area. Her essays and reviews have appeared in *Amerasia Journal*; *Rain Taxi Review of Books*; the anthology *Once Upon a Dream: Twenty Years of Vietnamese-American Experience* (Andrews and McMeel, 1995); Hop Luu Magazine and Viet Magnet. In addition, she is also working with in translating the poems of the Vietnamese poet Lam Thi My Da, who was a resident poet at the Joiner in the summer 2000 session. Their collaborated efforts have appeared on *Sante Fe Poetry Broadside* and *Vietnam Cultural Window.*

Lyn Doiron is a self-taught artist, writer, performer, and junk store enthusiast. She lives in Portland, Oregon, with her partner John, and is currently learning to fly by the seat of her pants.

On poetry and the writing community:

We live in a world that relentlessly bombards us with images and information, encourages us to move faster, acquire more, feel less. To survive in this landscape we tend to bar the windows. We lock up the heart for its protection and look suspiciously at anyone in our yard.

A poem doesn't knock. It walks right in through the front door of the heart, plops itself down on the couch and asks what's for dinner? It is when I invite others into that tender room that I discover it is more than exquisitely arranged words that connects us. No matter if it is a group of writers, gardeners or gossips, community is the key to opening to our humanness. I am grateful to the Joiner Center and to Fred Marchant in particular.

Lisa Fay has been writing for 30 years. Fay wrote in the beginning because she didn't always talk well. Now the Boston resident writes because she has meaningful things to say. She always wrote knowing she had the support of her family and now, many editors. She writes many human interest, family, and nature poems. Her artistic ambition has expanded to include painting and photography.

On poetry and the writing community:

The Joiner Center has been instrumental in helping me find mentors and publication outlets.

Sarah Furo was a runner up for the 1994 Grolier Poetry contest. Her poems have appeared in *Touchstone*, a British journal for the poetry and literature of the Order of Bards, Ovates and Druids. She is published in the anthology, *Ffytherau* (no, I don't know how to pronounce it), poetry inspired by earth spirituality. Her poetry has appeared for the last five years in the *Lunar Calendar*, published by Luna Press. Sarah attended the Joiner Center seminars in 1998 and 1999, and has met with other participants in bouts of all night poetry readings ever since. Sarah is a flower essence practitioner and astrologer. She combines these healing practices which come from earth and sky into what she calls, Star-Flower Alchemy. She teaches courses in Astrology, Tarot and Ogham, the Druid alphabet of the trees.

Pauline Hebert was a Captain in the US Army Nurse Corps at the 12th Evacuation Hospital in Chu Chi Vietnam from January of 1968 to December of 1968. She arrived in-country two weeks before the Tet Offensive. After two years of service she was honorably discharged in August of 1969. She earned a Masters of Science in Nursing and a Ph.D. in Education from the University of Connecticut. She retired from the Veterans Affairs Nursing Service in 1990. Pauline speaks at high schools and colleges telling students "It took me nine months to get the blood out from under my fingernails". She has attended the William Joiner Center Writer's Workshop. Her poetry has appeared in *The Boston Poet*, *From Both Sides Now: Poetry from Vietnam War and its Aftermath*, Ed: P. Mahony, Scribner's and will be in the June issue of *Rattle*. On line her poetry has appeared in *Poets on Line*. She currently lives in the Adirondacks of New York with her cat Sugar.

Preston H. Hood, III served with SEAL Team 2 in Vietnam. He is a self-taught brick and stonemason and carpenter. In 1973 he graduated from University of Massachusetts Boston with a BA in English, Magna Cum Laude. He received his Masters Degree in Special Education Administration from UMO in 1997. His poems have appeared in *ECHOES: A Journal of Northern Maine, Maine Times, The Worcester Review, PEACE IS OUR PROFESSION* Anthology, *The Journal of American Culture* and many other literary journals and online publications. Last year, he won an Honorable Mention for his poem "Salt & Dirt" in the Winter/Spring 2001, Issue No. 4 of *FLASH!POINT*. He has poems forthcoming in the *South Boston Literary Gazette Volume 4 and 5, Vietnam War Generation Journal* and *Animus # 6*.

For Veteran's Day, 2001, he was a featured reader at the William Joiner Center for War and Social Consequences at University of Massachusetts Boston.

On poetry and the writing community:

I began writing over thirty years ago because it made me feel better than I did when I did not write. Writing never cured all my woes, but it allowed me the chance to state my feelings and knowledge creatively in a way that caught people's attention. Before Vietnam, I muddled through the English Sonnets, Shakespeare and I wrote rhymed verse. After Vietnam, I read Whitman, Joyce, Yeats, Frost, Elliot, cummings and Thomas and became hooked on poetry. Since Vietnam changed me so profoundly, my writing has been my survival; it has been a way for me to move through dark and find light.

Overall, my writing teaches me a great deal about others and myself. It gives me the confidence to talk with words and bridge the vast silence between us all. When I complete a poem, whether it is written in a single draft or many drafts, it is a dance of sparks with a flame of fury. But most of all, it makes me feel darn good. It comes down to this: I want my poetry to be added to the consciousness of the world. My writing always gets me involved at some level with others. Through the writing process, word-talk lets us stand for the goodness of all man. Like the peace process, which happened in Northern Ireland, it is not about politics or who is right or wrong, but about how people live, love, laugh, cry and share their inner most strength about caring for others. Ultimately, it allows us to reconcile with the world.

Jacqueline M. Loring is a poet, writer and photographer who lives with her Vietnam veteran husband and their large blended family on the west coast of Cape Cod. She annually attends the Joiner Center Writers' Conference and the Cape Cod Writers' Center Writers' Conference. She has had several poems published including "Curse the Rainbow" that appeared in the Scribner anthology *From Both Sides Now: Poetry from Vietnam War and its Aftermath*, edited by Phillip Mahony.

Peg Mahoney, Braintree, received a B.A. in English from UMASS Boston. Her poems and essays have been published in *South Shore Anthology of Poets*, *Granite State News*, *Touchstone*, *West Crook Review*, *N.E. Writer's Magazine*, *Harp-Strings*

Journal. A staged reading of her play, <u>Patterns in Glass</u>, was presented at the Boston Center for the Arts. As a volunteer, Peg chairs the Site Selection Committee for South Shore Habitat for Humanity. Her favorite activity is swing dancing.

E. B. Moore came to writing full time through art-book building and metal sculpture. Short stints as an EMT, and a personal chef have also influence what she writes. Her work has been published in the *Charles River Review*, *The Brattler*, and *The Beacon Hill Times* as a literary prizewinner.

Dianne Collins Ouellette is a writer, teacher, mother, and survivor. Currently, she is pretending to work on her dissertation at UMASS Amherst in Rhetoric and Composition, and is teaching at the New England Institute of Art and Communication in Brookline.
She has published a chapbook of poems, <u>Several Summers,</u> and has had several other poems published, including two in <u>The South Boston Literary Gazette</u>. Her poetry is about life, simplicity, and the courage it takes to laugh while struggling forward. Dianne's new book of Poems, <u>Culling for Keepers</u>, is due out in the summer of 2002.
(Dianne C. Ouellette passed away on November 27, 2001, having written her last poem earlier that month.)

Candace Perry is a writer, activist, and social worker living in Wellfleet on Cape Cod. Her current writing projects include a collection of stories about growing up in the military and a full-length play which explores the conflicts presented in "Your Family." Among the many gifts in her life are a supportive spouse and the opportunity to have studied with Grace Paley over several years.

Vasco R. A. Pires is a Writer/Artist/Educator, born in Canton, Ohio, 1941. Graduate of Massachusetts College of Art, BSEd. 1971. Now retired from teaching, he devotes his time to perfecting his skills as a writer and visual artist. Between working on his first volume of poetry titled, "A Fraction of Me", he also produces a half hour TV Video documentary series, "A Fraction of Me". Vasco's objective is to work on planning and development of materials and events that reflect the unique contributions Capeverdeans have made to American culture. His commitment to work toward world peace and understanding between all people, through constructive dialogue through the medium of the arts.

On poetry and the writing community:

Attending work shops like the annual William Joiner Center' Writer's Conference, at U Mass. Boston, has provided me with inspiration and support from writers and poets from all over the world.

Gary Rafferty served in the US Army in Vietnam in 1970-71. He retired from the Nashua, New Hampshire Fire Department as a lieutenant in 1991. He lives in Hudson, NH with his sons, Ian and Shawn, his two dalmatians, Bowie and Star and the "First Dog" Spunky. His work has appeared in, *Rattapallex, Flash!Point*, and *Rattle*, his poetry was also published in the anthology, *From Both Sides Now*. His poem, *Spunky* and his essay on *Writing Trauma Poetry* has been accepted for publication in the June 2002 issue of *Rattle*. He has attended the William Joiner Centers Writer's Workshop every year since 1991.

Sue Roberts is a teacher and writer living in Boston for the past 17 years. She grew up in Vermont, which continues to be a focus of her work, and the tension between city and town. Her poems have appeared in *The Amethyst Review*, *Boston Poet*, *Revue Riviere*, *Oregon Review*, *Poetry Motel* and *Ceide Fields* (Ireland). She teaches writing and literature at Boston College, and is at work on a poetry manuscript and a collection of essays. She is entirely devoted to her terrier, Fergus, who appears in many of her poems and inspires all of them.

Maureen Ryberg was born in Ireland. Raised in England. Married an American on the Isle of Capri. Living happily ever after south of Boston. Finishing a novel set in Ireland between two World Wars. Publications include *Poet Lore* and *The Worcester Review*.

A Community of Words, A Circle of Poets

On poetry and the writing community:

Hard to believe it's been eleven years since I signed up for a Joiner Center Workshop with Yusef Komunyakaa after the Persian Gulf War of 1991 - the first war I had seen in living color on TV. The horror of that war spurred me into writing - first poems, then a novel that explores the effects of two world wars on a family in Ireland. I have learned from so many people, too numerous to mention. You know who you are. Sounds like a threat. It's supposed to be a sincere Thank You! I hope you'll be rewarded with dedications, epigraphs, acknowledgments, e.g., in my novel that awaits publication. Now, if you'd only give me the name of your agent...

MaryEdna Salvi make greeting cards, dabble a bit in painting. She is a singer and writes poetry "not as often as my soul needs it." She has a daughter-in-spirit, Molly, a son, Shantu and grandson, Tariq. She tries her best to be aware of the creative energy in and around my life.

On poetry and the writing community:

Several years ago when I first applied to the William Joiner Center, I wrote that, having sung over thirty years, I needed to start using my own words to express my feelings. Well, the workshops do just that. They teach me the techniques that help clarify my thoughts and emotions, so I can put them down on paper.
But, for me, more than writing poetry happens at the Center. The people there, the visiting faculty, students, and writing staff, by not only in giving of their love for words and truth, but, in the risks they take whenever one looks inward, encourages me to do the same. Which even goes beyond art. It's what living in this world is all about.

Catherine Sasanov is the author of two poetry collections: Traditions of Bread and Violence, published by Four Way Books; and All the Blood Tethers, the 2002 Morse Poetry Prize winner, forthcoming this fall from Northeastern University Press. She also authored the libretto for Las Horas de Belen: A Book of

170

Hours, commissioned by Mabou Mines. The theater piece received a special citation for performance at the 2000 Village Voice Obie Awards.

Steffanie Schwam is a nurse who works in a newborn intensive care unit in Boston. Her poetry has appeared in *Neshama, a journal of jewish women's spirituality.* Steffanie also plays folk harp.

Carmi Soifer lives with her daughter, Tailia, in Cambridge, MA. She teaches writing through 'WritingWorks' and in community settings.

Cornelia Veenendaal has published three books of poetry and is working on a fourth. She taught at the University of Massachusetts Boston until her retirement, and was a founding member of Alice James Books.

Dorinda Foley Wegener annually studies poetry at the William Joiner Center Writer's Conference where she has worked along side Bruce Weigl, John Deane, and Eva Bourke. Her work has appeared in *The Larcom Review* and *Ceide*, as well as many other local publications. Her poems have won numerous awards and honors including the *Writers Harvest: National Reading.*

On poetry and the writing community:

As for the instructors at the Center... I would say the reason I enjoy the Joiner Center is the unconditional support for the poet and their work on all levels, whether emotionally, physically, mentally, etc. given by the instructors. Each instructor has helped me directly with my own voice. Eva, The blessed Mother of poetry, has helped me emotionally, by creating an environment were I could realize that what I have to say is valuable and not to give up on myself. Bruce has taught me to be mentally aware - pay attention to form and look for the magic in language (I am still NOT going to write a sonnet). And John, closest to my heart, has helped me keep my feet on the ground, to pay attention to the physical, write what I know, and accept the iconography in my work as beautiful, not a hindrance. Everyday he challenged me beyond what I thought I could write or turn out. And most of all, he accepted my anger and frustration over the whole writing process with a good sense of humor and a pint. The instructors are definitely what keep me returning to the Joiner Center.

Acknowledgments

Alice Barton
"Words for You, Mother" <u>Atlantic Review</u> Vol. 8.1, Fall/Winter (2001): 98.

Dave Connolly
"Food For Thought, 3 AM" <u>Lost in America</u> Ed. David Connolly. Viet Nam Generation, Inc & Burning Cities Press, 1994
"Come On Home" <u>South Boston Literary Gazette</u> Vol. 5. Summer (2001). 14.
"To the Vietnamese Veterans" <u>South Boston Literary Gazette</u> Vol. 5. Summer (2001): <u>23.</u>

Carmi Soifer
"Poet" <u>Between the Sounds Anthology</u>, Vol 2. Spring (2000).

Jacqueline M. Loring
"Tender Morsels" <u>The Boston Poet</u>, August. 1997.
"The Test" <u>The Boston Poet</u>, August. 1997.

Dianne Collins Ouellette
"Sinner in the Hands" <u>Several Summers.</u> Ed. Dianne Collins Ouellette. Small Poetry Press, 1998.
"Apogee" <u>Several Summers</u>, Small Poetry Press, 1998.

Dorinda Foley Wegener
"Mary to Her Brother" <u>The Larcom Review</u> Vol 3.1. (2001): 97, 107.

Index

This anthology is more than a gathering of poems and poets. It is a convergence of paths, a literary labyrinth, and an honoring of the written word. *Summer Home Review* is the work of nurses, firemen, high school and college teachers, healers, artists, soldiers, lawyers, singers, union members, and entrepreneurs whose poems and stories are included. While it is true that some of the poets are Vietnam veterans, their poems are not necessarily "war" poems. The reader will find that poets other than veterans write about battles. Though the poets/writers in this anthology have all participated in the same workshop, this book is neither "war" poetry nor writing that is of "workshop" quality.

All the poems in *Summer Home Review* have an edge. Poems by Dorinda Foley Wegener will delight some and poems by Gary Rafferty may infuriate or sadden others but all the poems and stories are compelling.

Through the book you can trace the literary bonds and friendships of the poets and find the influences of their poet-teachers like Bruce Weigl, Fred Marchant, Yusef Komunyakaa, Lady Borton, Bill Ehrhart, and others.

Like travelers in a labyrinth, the poets and writers included in *Summer Home Review* have reached the center and, with publication of this book are making their way back to the beginning. This book begins for you at the center. The editor, poet Jacqueline M. Loring, invites you to walk back with them. "In between the lines." she says, "they have left for you sacred pieces of themselves. Enjoy the journey.

"The writer believes strongly in the ability to use words to persuade the reader, to evoke emotions, to extract humor, and to entertain. *Summer Home Review* brings this revelation to anyone who will read and listen."

Richard Berred Ouellette

Editor's Biography

Jacqueline M. Loring

Jacqueline Loring is a poet, writer and photographer who lives on the west side of Cape Cod with her husband and their large, blended family. She was married in July of 1969 to Warren Gary Loring after his tour in the Delta of Vietnam from Christmas 1967 to Christmas 1968 with the U. S. Army MASH Hospital.

Jacqueline was an obstetrical nurse for almost twenty years and in 1972 she was the first staff nurse hired by a Cape Cod hospital to teach the Lamaze Method of Prepared Childbirth. From 1987 to 1993 she was employed as the Maternal Child Health Specialist at Visions Teen Parent Home in South Yarmouth, Massachusetts. She served as the program director from 1993 to 1998 when she retired to write full time. Jacqueline, who has a Master's Degree in Management, is presently the Executive Director of the Cape Cod Writers' Center.

Her poetry has appeared in journals and magazines including CapeWomen and Prime Time, and Veterans for Peace and in two anthologies: *World War II Remembered, An Anthology*, and *From Both Sides Now: Poetry from Vietnam War and its Aftermath*, Scribner's, edited by Philip Mahony. She has read at the Katherine Lee Bates Poetry Festival in Falmouth Massachusetts and at the Brookline Booksmith, Brookline, Massachusetts. She reads with veterans at

"*Moving Wall*" events and at ceremonies that recognize the contributions of veterans. Her poetry brings the voice of the wife of a Vietnam veteran to the listener and to the reader.

Jacqueline is an avid photographer and in 1999 several of her photos appeared with her poems at the Ghost Ranch Painter's exhibit at the Cataumet Arts Center.

She has written two screenplays and is working on the institutional memoir of Cape Cod Hospital. In 2000, she was accepted as a member of the National League of American Pen Women.

About the Author

Summer Home Review is more than a gathering of poems and poets. It is a convergence of paths, a literary labyrinth, and an honoring of the written word. While it is true that some of the poets are Vietnam veterans, their poems are not necessarily "war" poems. The reader will find that poets other than veterans write about battles. Though the poets/writers in this anthology have all participated in the same workshop, this book is neither "war" poetry nor writing that is of "workshop" quality.

All the poems in Summer Home Review have an edge. Poems by Dorinda Foley Wegener will delight some and poems by Gary Rafferty may infuriate or sadden others but all the poems and stories are compelling.

Through the book you can trace the literary bonds and friendships of the poets and find the influences of their poet-teachers like Bruce Weigl, Fred Marchant, Yusef Komunyakaa, Lady Borton, Bill Ehrhart, Martha Collins and others.

Like travelers in a labyrinth, the poets and writers included in Summer Home Review have reached the center and, with publication of this book are making their way back to the beginning. This book begins for you at the center. The editor, poet Jacqueline M. Loring, invites you to walk back with them. "In between the lines." she says, "they have left for you sacred pieces of themselves.

"The writer believes strongly in the ability to use words to persuade the reader, to evoke emotions, to extract humor, and to entertain. Summer Home Review brings this revelation to anyone who will read and listen." Richard Berred Ouellette